THE EFFECTIVE GOSPEL SINGER

by APOSTLE (REV) T.T. CHIVAVIRO

PUBLISHED BY :

ASSEMBLIES OF PENTECOSTAL METHODISTS

(APM) LITERATURE DEPARTMENT

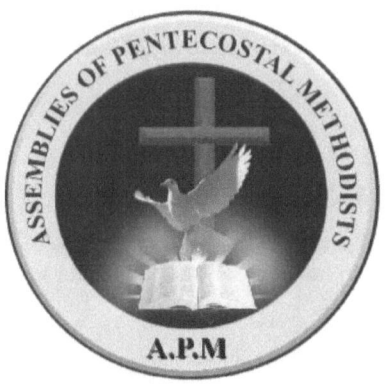

THE EFFECTIVE GOSPEL SINGER

p&c 2018 Rev T T Chivaviro

app : 0027789199381

office : +27 11 825 6525

email : pastortoggie@gmail.com

CONTENTS

CHAPTER 1

MY MUSICAL JOURNEY SO FAR

I have always longed to one day sit and put my musical story on paper, but it's too long to be contained in one book. Perhaps one day I will do an autobiography as I feel I have a lot to say to the posterity before I'm called home to rest finally. I believe this book may be just some very little contribution to the music industry, especially for those still learning the ropes of the trade.

I have always wondered what we could have avoided or how short our paths into the industry would have been , had those who started long before us, put to paper what they experienced, let alone what they went through to be the heroes we always admire. The sad part of it is all we have remaining are their timeless hits and classics, and nothing more. We would have greatly cherished the stories behind such classics, and it would probably have been easier for us to follow their paths.

This perhaps takes us to the purpose of this book. I may fail to exhaust all that's on my mind or all that musical beginners may want, but all I will try and do is pour my heart out in a way that may help someone out there. I will pour my research skills out in a way that may also save someone the hustle of torch-lighting in order to find their way in. The information contained here-in can only be a starting point. There's more that's happening in the music industry and trends are changing very fast. These basics can only be applied contextually and if this information will help someone get a foothold then glory be unto Jesus

My musical journey began in the remote village of Gwehava, 6km south of the now Gokwe Town Centre, in the Midlands Province of Zimbabwe. My late father, Mr Joice Chivaviro who was a chorister himself, would sit and sing with the whole family, my mother (the late May Havadi) my brothers (Machaya and Tazvarwa) and my sisters (Tsungirirai, Ropafadzo and the late Nyevero). We would not only sing church hymns, but even schools set piece competition songs. As a renowned PRIMARY School Head who taught in a number of schools in Gokwe he would bring the competition pieces and start by teaching the family first. In the process we all got to understand and read tonic-sol-fa notation songs. This resulted in all of us getting into school choirs at tender ages; I used to practice with the Rumhumha (Chegama) Primary School Choir when I was just 7 and in Grade two! When we transferred to the nearby Gwehava Primary School I joined the choir in Grade three. Other learners used to laugh at me as I was a tiny bodied boy who needed about 3 to four inside shorts just for the choir uniform to fit. This however did not discourage me as the teachers, Mr Jamela and Mr Bandawa, a year later began to ask me to assist them in conducting the school choir. It wasn't a big challenge since my father was teaching us all the basics, as well as music reading when we went back home. Because of this background, all the family members became choir directors and conductors at some point or the other, with some still leading church choirs wherever they go.

With this kind of foundation I grew up a very passionate chorister. Even when I moved to Moleli Secondary in Makwiro in 1988, I was already a choir member in the first week of school, becoming an assist to choir director to the late Mrs Nechibvute, a couple of weeks later until I left in 1991.Then we had formed a Trio that had myself, my brother Machaya and one Wilson Chindeka, we called it THE 3 BROTHERS. It was a vocal trio.

In 1992 I moved to Ellis Robins High School in Mabelreign, Harare where I not only became part of the school choirs but began to assist Mrs Coid in helping other boys read music notes. At the same time I joined the Mabelreign Methodist Choir and began to also assist Mr Muganyi and Mr Chisvo as one of the Choir Directors

It was in 1993 when the big move into instrumental music happened! We used to have scripture union meetings and the likes of Pastor G (Stanley Gwanzura) and Rita Shonhiwa would come and sing for us now and again, I used to love their sessions. However it was in October of the same year when we held our Scripture Union Concert that featured the late gospel great Brian Sibalo. He heard me singing with my partners Joel Alferi and Medicine Sayidi. He then took me aside and told me how my deep voice was like his and invited me to some of his concerts for me to learn. That was the time I began to follow the free concerts usually done in the Harare Gardens and met some renowned artists like baba Mechanic Manyeruke and the Family Singers under Shuvai Wutawunashe.

Two years later I was back in rural Gokwe as a teacher at Batanai Secondary, but the seed had already been planted, I wanted to do more than just choral music. Yes I directed the school choirs at the schools where I taught around, the likes of Muyambi, Karova, Mapfumo and Kangula, but I wanted more. I bought a small keyboard that I taught myself to play around 1996.Then I had lost touch with Brian although he was now a household name whose music I would buy at whatever cost .Armed with the small keyboard, I began to write songs both for choral and instrumental presentations.

1998 I moved into the United Theological College for theological training, having joined fulltime ministry in the Methodist Church in 1997.It was at that College where I immediately formed a group made up of student Pastors, Ossah Manyeza, Memory Chikosi, Kundai Marimbire and Loveness Madzoke. We were joined by Allen Dzobo (now my manager) on the Keyboards and Zivai Kamusasa on the drums, after meeting the two at Inner City United Methodist. I called this band THE FAITH AMBASSADORS.After marrying Juliet Chabata in 1998, she also joined the band. (God has blessed us with two kids Tinashe the boy born in 2003 and Munashe the girl born in 2006)

This is the team that recorded our first album, Peace Hope and Love at the late Tendai Mupfurutsa's High-Density Studios. The 6 track album was produced there by Mupfurutsa himself engineered by Noel Zembe, Clancy Mbirimi, Dickson Mandota and the late Adam Msindo.Thus began the journey that produced the following albums:**1999**: Peace ,Hope and Love, **2000**: Power, **2002**: Komborerai Africa, **2005**: Kuna Mwari

Zvitaure (Hymnal Praise Vol 1), **2006**: the Best Of (Compilation), **2009**: The Return, **2010**: Nguva Yakanakisisa (Hymnal Praise Vol 2), **2013**: To God Be The Glory (Hymnal Praise Vol 3), **2014**: Ishe Taungana (Hymnal Worship Vol 4), **2015** :EBENEZER-Tiri Munyasha, **2016** : Mhepo Inoperekedza & Tsitsi Dzake Ihuru, **2017** : Maranatha & The Best of (Vol 2), **2018** : Matishamisa Jireh

This journey has seen me sharing the stage with renowned gospel artists from southern Africa like Mechanic Manyeruke, Brian Sibalo, Baba namai Charamba, Fungisai, Pastor Haisa, Takesure Zama, Minister Mahendere, Blessing Shumba, Matthias Mhere, Saba Magacha, Rebecca Malope, Sipho Makhabane, Lundi, Vuyo Mokoena, Itani Madima,Pastor Benjamin Dube, Pastor Solly Mahlangu, Mahalia just to mention a few.

Although things were difficult and tough for me prior to 2016, I kept telling myself whatever I was doing was good enough. I had so many people in church feeling encouraged especially by the way we did hymnal renditions and that kept me going.

TURNAROUND :The big breakthrough came with the mass collaboration effort released in 2016,

EBENEZER TIRIMUNYASHA .I received this song in a dream and went on to record it ,featuring baba Charamba, baba Manyeruke, Pastor Haisa, Bethen Pasinawako Ngolomi, Rumbi Zvirikuzhe, Kudzi Nyakudya, Noel Zembe and my wife Juliet. The song just went viral, and it's a pity at a time when piracy raised its ugly head in Zimbabwe. It has become more like a "second national anthem" in the country and has won us several Awards and opened so many doors for us. It clocked over2 million views on YouTube in no time becoming the most viewed local gospel track in Zimbabwe.

From then on we have really started to enjoy the fruits of all those years of perseverance and not giving up. I have also done 2 other mass Collabos and I always enjoy it when I work together with so many artists in a single project.

AWARDS AND NOMINATIONS

2003: Musica Peace Award for music that promotes peace (for the song Runyararo from Komborerai Africa Album) shared with the late Ephat Mujuru and Alick Macheso.

2010: Nominated at the SABC Crown Gospel Awards in the Best Of Africa Category.

2015: 3 Awards,4 Nominations at the PERMICAN ZIMBABWE GOSPEL MUSIC AWARDS for the song Ebenezer : Song of the Year, Best Song Writer and Best

Produced Album of the year.End of the year EBENEZER number 1 on Starfm Gospel Greats top 50, as well as YaFm Gospel top 50 and Mixed top 100.It also came 3rd on Cocacola Radio Zimbabwe top 50 mixed and same position National Fm top 50 mixed the ONLY song to feature in the TOP THREE of ALL the country's major radio stations end of year charts.

2016: TRUMPET AFRICA GOSPEL AWARDS (TAGMA) Best Collaboration Award, nomination Best Traditional Gospel

2016: SABC Crown Gospel Awards BEST OF AFRICA Award

2017:4 Nominations at the RSA Ingoma Gospel Awards, 2 Nomiations ZimbabweMusicAwards (ZIMA), 2 Nominations NAMA Awards.Starfm End ofYear Award for MHEPO INOPEREKEDZA

2018 release, Matishamisa Jireh breaks the weekly Cococola Top 20 CHARTS record by clocking over 24000 votes in a week; this is the biggest combined Chart Show in Zimbabwe at the moment.

Music has taken us to several countries such as Botswana, Mozambique, Zambia, France, United Kingdom, Israel, Netherlands, and United Arab Emirates As I write this we are preparing for our first USA performance towards the end of the year

My musical journey in full needs a whole book on its own; soon I will be working on that autobiography.

When I look at all these, including my background and where I have come from in the industry, I see the hand of God and celebrate his Grace. At some point I remember some close friends saying my voice was not suitable for instrumental music, while some said I should try to sing like some artists they preferred. In 2005 as I was completing my Masters Studies at the University of Zimbabwe some also suggested I quit music since it was for "the less educated" but I just wouldn't. I have learnt a lot of lessons along the way and some of the lessons are what I will share with you in this book. Most of the information is gathered out that experience and what PATIENCE has taught me in music ministry

It's so sad my music teacher, my father passed on before he could also enjoy the BIG TURNAROUND , and my mother also passed on in 1993 before I had even recorded anything. I'm sure they would have loved seeing the result of their many years musical instruction .I have never attended any formal music school so far, maybe will do so soon, but all I'm relying on are years learning from others and what my own father deposited unto me in terms of tutelage.MAY GOD USE WHAT I WILL WRTITE HERE TO TURN AROUND SOMEBODY'S MUSICAL ASSIGNMENT!

CHAPTER 2

WHAT IS GOSPEL MUSIC

As we feel called to preach the gospel through music or as we partake in the process of singing gospel music, we need to understand the fundamentals of this type.

Gospel music cannot be categorised as a genre perse, because in layman terms genre has to do mainly with the accompanying type of music for example Reggae, Rock, Blues, House, and Kwaito etc. As I will explain soon, you will find a gospel song accompanied by traditional mbira, a gospel song done in dancehall style, reggae or even rap gospel!

Gospel is in some spheres referred to as Christian music. The moment we categorise it as Gospel or Christian, we are already aligning it to Jesus Christ, the one to whom THE GOSPEL is all about. This is the only type of music that "has an owner".

Once one decides to sing this type of music then you automatically have to refer to what the owner wants and prescribes. Therefore for us to understand better what Gospel music is all about, we need to understand what THE GOSPEL is first. Old English gōdspel, from gōd 'good' + spel 'news, a story' (see spell), translating ecclesiastical Latin bona annuntiatio. The GOOD NEWS that is attested in John 3:16 , *" **For God so loved the world that he gave his only begotten son that whosoever believeth in him should not perish but have eternal life.."***

gospel'gɒsp(ə)l/ noun

the teaching or revelation of Christ.

"it is the Church's mission to preach the gospel"

synonyms: Christian teaching, Christ's teaching, the life of Christ, the word of God, the good news, Christian doctrine, the New Testament, the writings of the evangelists

the record of Christ's life and teaching in the first four books of the New Testament.

Meaning if this is what THE GOSPEL is all about then it should make it easier therefore to understand what gospel music is.

According to Wikipedia, *Gospel music is Christian music. The creation, performance, significance, and even the definition of gospel music varies according to culture and social context. ....*

This points to the fact that we cannot talk of music being GOSPEL if it has no attachment to the "owner of the Gospel". Would this then mean it's all about the New Testament? A big NOOO to that! As much as we have the old testament and the New Testament letters all linked to Christ in one way or the other as part of one whole salvific narrative, so is the music that is aligned to the story.

I have often challenged Gospel artists to say, after composing your song, go through it again and show us where God is in the song, show us where Jesus is, in the song. If they are nowhere to be found there-in, it's difficult for me to classify your song as a gospel song.

In this manner, it also means classifying yourself as a gospel artist does not therefore mean every song that you write or sing is gospel. For me, it's not about WHO has sung the song, The Gospel is a message, its news. GOSPEL IS NOT A BEAT OR RHYTHM, ITS A MESSAGE. Therefore you may find a generally "non-gospel" artist singing a gospel song. The instruments used for the music accompanying a gospel song may vary from traditional to modern, styles varying too from up-tempo to slow melodies. What matters is what you open your mouth to say or sing.

Then there's the issue of using instruments and dances to accompany gospel music in the churches. This issue has become very controversial on its own, and in this book, soon in this chapter we shall see why. Musical history shows that music actually developed from the church, and was later on adopted by pagan idol worshippers. As a result the church then at some point tried to dissociate itself from pagan practices and this ended up with people thinking music and dancing were pagan practices!

Perhaps the best way to understand it is maybe looking the history and development of gospel music.

GOSPEL MUSIC HISTORY AND DEVELOPMENT

Let's look at this according to LaSaundra Booth, a licensed Music Educator with eleven years of teaching experience, and a Master's degree in Music Education.

"Have you ever heard a song that moved you to the point where you wanted to tell all of your friends about it? Well, that's the type of feeling you may experience when listening to gospel music. By its very definition, the term gospel means 'good news.' Gospel music is one of the vehicles through which the ideals of Christianity have been spread to audiences all over the world."

History

Gospel music may be traced back to the days of creation when angels would praise and worship God before that task was bestowed upon humanity. According to historian Robert Lockyer, a look at the Old

Testament reveals how God's ancient people were devoted to the study and practice of music, which holds a unique place in the historical and prophetic books, as well as the Psalter."

The music of religious ritual was first used by King David, and, according to the Larousse Encyclopedia of Music, he is credited with confirming the men of the Tribe of Levi as the "custodians of the music of the divine service."

The study of ancient musical instruments has been practiced for centuries with some researchers studying instruments from Israel/Palestine dating to the biblical period. Archaeological and written data have demonstrated clearly that music was an integral part of daily life in ancient Israel/Palestine. Egypt was among the oldest cultures of the Near East and had a highly developed musical culture dating back to around 3000 BC. Egyptian sources, however, include only pictorial relics, some instruments, and a few literary records concerned with performance practices. On various pieces of sculpture there are reliefs of harpists and flutists taking part in religious ceremonies and social entertainments.

Although records are minimal, it is known that between 3000 and 2300 BC organized temple music with singers existed in Sumer and Babylonia, the oldest cultural groups in Mesopotamia. Excavations have uncovered several musical instruments, including harps, lutes, double oboes, and a few others.

The musical traditions of the Temple were rudely broken by the destruction of the First Temple and the exile of the Jews in Babylon during the 6th century BC. Hindley notes that most of the psalms seem to have been written in the years after the return of the Jews to Jerusalem. At this time too, the practice of antiphonal singing between the cantor and the congregation seems to have become common. The musical art of the Levites, the Temple musicians who were named after their historic ancestors, was lost by the end of the 1st century.

In 70 AD the Second Temple was destroyed by the troops of the Emperor Titus and in the years following the Levites along with the majority of Jews fled from Palestine. As a result, the synagogue music of the Dispersion lost the joyful character of that of the Temple and the large instrumental forces were dispensed with.

The New Testament was not written until centuries later than the old and the music had attained much higher development, according to music historian Ida Whitcomb. As it related to Christ, it is called Christian music. **It's interesting to note that Jesus Christ and his disciples also sang hymns, Matthew 26:30 records- Then they sang a hymn** and went out to the Mount of Olives. ...near to Jerusalem and came to Bethphage on the Mount of Olives.

There are but few allusions to Christian music in three of the Gospels: in the Gospel of Luke, there are the "Angels' Song," Mary's "Magnificat," and Zacharias's "Song." In Acts, Paul and Silas sing behind prison-bars: the prison is shaken, the doors fly open, and they are free. In the Epistles, there are but few references to music, but in Ephesians there is a "beautiful one," in which Paul exhorts the churches to sing "Psalms" and "spiritual songs."

Hindley adds that antiphonal chants between cantor or priest and the congregation originated in Hebrew worship methods. At its peak around the beginning of the Christian era, the elaborate music of the Temple was performed by a large choir of highly trained men singers, with boys sometimes added, and during this period many instruments also were used by the Temple orchestra

Whitcomb adds that many of our noblest Church hymns have been suggested by the Psalms, which she notes was the first hymn-book of the Hebrew nation and remains today not only the hymn-book of the Hebrew Temple, but also of the Christian Church.

Gospel music as we have it now, is deeply rooted in the rich traditions of the African-American church. During the late 1800s, African-American churches in the southern United States started fusing various styles of music into their worship services, including African-American spirituals, hymns, and sacred songs. Such music was primarily sung at church and accompanied by hand-clapping and foot-stomping.

At the heart of the gospel music tradition was the use of a choir. The church choir consisted of a group of volunteer singers from the church congregation. Choir members could easily be distinguished from the rest of the congregation because they normally dressed in uniforms, which were choir robes. This might be something you remember from various films like The Blues Brothers, Sister Act 2, or Norbit. The types of music sung by the gospel choir followed the call-and-response format similar to that used in traditional hymns and sacred songs.

The traditional structure of gospel music changed in the late 1930s when Thomas A. Dorsey, who became known as the 'Father of Gospel Music,' began working for Pilgrim Baptist Church in Chicago, Illinois. Dorsey was a former jazz pianist and composer who had worked with famous players such as Ma Rainey and Hudson Tamp Red Whitaker. Dorsey created a new style of gospel music called gospel blues, which infused his study of blues and jazz with traditional gospel music. It was initially rejected; however, by the end of the 1930s, gospel blues won over acceptance as the new form of traditional gospel.

Gospel music continued to evolve throughout the late 1930s. There are four distinct styles of gospel music including, but not limited to, quartet style, traditional gospel, contemporary gospel, and praise and worship.

The gospel quartet style is one in which a small number of male vocalists sing music together with tight harmonies. The major difference between traditional and contemporary gospel styles is that while traditional gospel usually features a more basic sound suited for singing by a choir, contemporary gospel places more emphasis on solo artists. Most contemporary artists rarely sing with a choir.

Prior to then, the term "Gospel music" was not used. Instead, people referred to "Gospel hymns" — stately, dignified religious songs with definite references to the Gospel message of the New Testament. One of the earliest of these Gospel hymns goes back to 1529, when Martin Luther wrote the words and composed the music of the stately and much sung A Mighty Fortress is our God. The theme of the hymn is "relying on Jesus Christ to overcome the Devil," with specific references to Psalm 46, Galatians 5:22, and Philippians 2:9-10. This is not, however, the kind of music we think of today as Gospel music.

In the mid-1800s two men developed a new kind of religious music that was to become today's Gospel music. The two men were famed evangelist Dwight L. Moody and his music director and soloist, Ira D. Sankey, known as the "Sweet Singer."

Sankey's music was definitely different from traditional church music, and today's classic Gospel music has these same qualities as his music. The term **"Gospel Music"** first appeared in print in 1874 in a songbook named Gospel Songs: A Choice Collection of Hymns and Tunes.

We may go on to look at the history and development of Gospel music in various continents, but that's a subject for another day. As missionaries took the Gospel around continents so did the music develop and grow in those continents as well.

Interestingly most of the worship spirituals are said to have been developed during the slave trade era and they became known widely as "negro-spirituals". Most of the "negro-spirituals'" text are based on the Old Testament. There was a strong identification with Moses leading his people out of Egypt, out of bondage. And so that possibly may be one of the reasons. The gospel, on the other hand, is about the good news, about Christ coming again. Much of it is based on the New Testament. There are some other factors, too, that

I think are important and one of the things that was not looked upon with great favor during the period of enslavement was the use of instruments. There was this fear that instruments could be used to communicate and inspire uprisings. Drums were actually banned. And that played a critical role in how rhythm developed among African-Americans in the United States. But although the drums were banned, there were surrogates. One of the primary surrogates to create rhythms were hand-clapping and foot-stamping."

"One of the things that eventually evolved out of this is the use of refrain lines. It's important to remember that a lot of the folks who attended these services could read. So audience participation or communal participation, which is conceptually a very African thing, was something that was important to them in their services and that became a part of what they did."

We could go on and on, but for the purposes of our intent in this book, we will close this development at this point

Some may use gospel music to preach the gospel of Jesus Christ itself, while others may use gospel music to uplift and encourage souls. Some may use gospel music to praise and worship their creator, God the Father, yet others may use it as an art, a source of livelihood. USAGE OF GOSPEL MUSIC IS USUALLY CONTEXTUAL, BUT GOSPEL MUSIC HAS TO BE ABOUT THE GOSPEL, AND THE GOSPEL IS THE MESSAGE!

CHAPTER 3

THE POWER OF PRAISE AND WORSHIP

Let us begin by taking a look at this.

Acts 16:23-26 "And when they had laid many stripes on them, they threw them into prison, commanding the jailer to keep them securely.

(24) Having received such a charge, he put them into the inner prison and fastened their feet in the stocks.

(25) But at midnight Paul and Silas were praying and singing hymns to God, and the prisoners were listening to them.

(26) Suddenly there was a great earthquake, so that the foundations of the prison were shaken; and

immediately all the doors were opened and everyone's chains were loosed."

This Bible story begins the unjust arrest of Paul and Silas. Because they had cast a spirit of divination out of a girl, the local Philippian authorities beat them and then threw them into a jail cell. Besides the trauma of the severe beating, they were fastened in stocks which clamped their arms and legs in an immobile position, causing cramps and loss of circulation. The atmosphere there was depressing. According to the standards of that day, a prison was more like the resemblance of a dungeon. A dark, damp, stench-ridden place, with no facility for waste or comforts of any kind.

Yet, in spite of the throbbing pain in their bodies and the disheartening atmosphere, at midnight Paul and Silas were heard praying and singing praises to God! What a strange sound this must have been to the other prisoners, who were used to only hearing the groans or cursings of those who had been beaten.

Then suddenly, there was an earthquake that shook the prison! The doors flung open, and amazingly, the bonds of Paul, Silas, and every other prisoner were released! What caused this mighty discharge of power?

Praise Elevates us into God's Presence and Power

Paul and Silas knew the secret of how to lift their hearts above their troubles and enter into God's presence and power. Through praise and worship their hearts were raised into the joyous presence and peace of God, and provided God a channel for his power to operate in their circumstances.

The Bible says that God inhabits in the praises of His people (Psalms 22:3). In other words, God "dwells" in the atmosphere of His praise. This means that praise is more than a reaction of coming into His presence... praise to God is a vehicle of faith which takes us into His presence and power! Praise and worship is the "gate-pass" which allows us to enter the sacredness of His glory. The psalmist writes, "Enter into his gates with thanksgiving, and into his courts with praise: be thankful unto him, and bless his name" (Psalms 100:4).

This corresponds with Jesus' teaching, that His presence will inhabit the gathering of believers who congregate in His name: "For where two or three are gathered together in my name, there am I in the midst of them" (Matthew 18:20). A "gathering in His name" means that Jesus must be the focus, the center of the assemblage. He must be the one preached about, sung about — the one praised and worshiped. "I will declare thy name unto my brethren, in the midst of the church will I sing praise unto thee" (Hebrews 2:12). Consequently, Christ's presence, along with His virtue and anointing, is manifested in this type of gathering.

Have you ever noticed when "gifts of the Spirit" operate in a church service? The power and anointing of the Holy Spirit usually becomes evident, subsequent to a time of worship and praise. Some think that worship is a response after the Holy Spirit moves upon them. However, it's the other way around. God's presence responds when we move upon Him with worship! Lifting up Jesus Christ through praise and worship invokes the Lord's presence and power to flow in our midst.

What is Praise?

Praise means "to commend, to applaud or magnify." For the Christian, praise to God is an expression of worship, lifting-up and glorifying the Lord. It is an expression of humbling ourselves and centering our attention upon the Lord with heart-felt expressions of love, adoration and thanksgiving. High praises bring our spirit into a pinnacle of fellowship and intimacy between ourselves and God — it magnifies our awareness of our spiritual union with the most high God. Praise transports us into the realm of the supernatural and into the power of God. "Blessed is the people that know the joyful sound: they shall walk, O LORD, in the light of thy countenance" (Psalms 89:15).

Two Hebrew words are used for Praise and these are **Yadah** and **Towdah**. Yadah is defined as: To give thanks, laud or praise. An expression of thank or praise in ritual, public and personal praise. It is found mostly in

the book of psalms, some 70 times. (Dan 2:23 NASB)
*"To Thee, O God of my fathers, I give thanks (yada)
and praise, for Thou hast given me wisdom and power;
Even now Thou hast made known to me what we
requested of Thee, for Thou hast made known to us the
king's matter."*

Yadah comes from the root YAD meaning hand. Yadah
then is to throw out the hands, or extend the hands in
the giving of thanks as part of our worship experience.
Yadah praise is one in which we raise our hands in an
outburst of spontaneous gratitude for what God has
done. Our hands are used as an extension of our
expression of thanks. One may also express thankful
praise on a musical instrument.

Towdah is a confession of faith that God is supreme
and able to do all things. Towdah also means
thanksgiving, associated with sacrificing, was used of
choirs or processions.Itss used as: confession, hymns
of thanksgiving, praise, sacrifice of thanksgiving, thank
offering.This type of offering means we will not consider
our circumstances with our natural eyes, but we look

only through the eyes of faith at our God our deliverer. Towdah is not to be underestimated as it will move the hand of God upon our lives. It believes God for the impossible and releases the power and wisdom of God on our behalf as we praise (Towdah) Him.

There are many actions involved with praise to God — verbal expressions of adoration and thanksgiving, singing, playing instruments, shouting, dancing, lifting or clapping our hands. But true praise is not "merely" going through these motions. Jesus spoke about the hypocrisy of the Pharisees, whose worship was only an outward show and not from the heart. "This people draweth nigh unto me with their mouth, and honoureth me with their lips; but their heart is far from me" (Matthew 15:8). Genuine praise to God is a matter of humility and sincere devotion to the Lord from within.

Unpretentious praise pleases the Lord. He delights in the love and devotion of His children. According to the scriptures, the various expressions of praise bring blessing to the Lord. He eagerly awaits the fragrance of our affections, desiring to manifest His sweet presence and power in our midst. "...the true worshipers shall worship the Father in spirit and in truth: for the Father seeketh such to worship him" (John 4:23).

Praise to God is a Lifestyle

All too often, praise to God is something that many people leave at church, an event that happens only when they come together with other Christians. However, praise should be a part of a believers lifestyle, inter-mingled as a part of their daily prayer-life. At work, in the car, at home in bed, or anywhere; praise to the Lord brings the refreshing of the Lord's presence, along with His power and anointing. "...I will bless the LORD at all times: his praise shall continually be in my mouth" (Psalms 34:1).

Praise is an expression of faith, and a declaration of victory! It declares that we believe God is with us and is in control of the outcome of all our circumstances (Romans 8:28). Praise is a "sacrifice," something that we offer to God sacrificially, not just because we feel like it, but because we believe in Him and wish to please Him. "By him therefore let us offer the sacrifice of praise to God continually, that is, the fruit of our lips giving thanks to his name" (Hebrews 13:15).

Praise Sends the Enemy Running

Since praise manifests God's presence, we also realize that praise repels the presence of the enemy, Satan. An atmosphere which is filled with sincere worship and praise to God by humble and contrite hearts is disgusting to the Devil. He fears the power in the name of Jesus, and flees from the Lord's habitation in praise. "Whoso offereth praise glorifieth me: and to him that ordereth his conversation aright will I show the salvation of God" (Psalms 50:23).

When the children of Judah found themselves outnumbered by the hostile armies of Ammon, Moab, and mount Seir, King Jehoshophat and all the people sought the Lord for His help. The Lord assured the people that this would be His battle. He told them to go out against them, and He would do the fighting for them. So what did the children of Judah do? Being the people of "praise" (Judah actually means Praise), and knowing that God manifests His power through praise, they sent their army against their enemies, led by the praisers!

So on they went, ahead of the army declaring, *"Praise the Lord, for His mercy endureth forever!"* And the scripture says, "...when they began to sing and to praise, the LORD set ambushments against the children of Ammon, Moab, and mount Seir, which were come against Judah; and they were smitten" (2 Chronicles 20:22).

When God's people begin to praise His name, it sends the enemy running! I challenge you to become a person of praise, and you will experience the release of the power of God!

Some Biblical Expressions of Praise

Declaring of thanks (Heb. 13:15)

Clapping hands and shouting (Psalms 47:1)

Musical instruments and dancing (Psm. 150:4)

Singing praise songs (Psalms 9:11)

Psalms, hymns, & spiritual songs (Eph. 5:19-20)

Making a joyful noise (Psalms 98:4)

By lifting our hands (Psalms 134:2)

By being still (Psalms 4:3-5, 46:10)

By being loud (Psalms 33:3, 95:1-6)

8 things that Praise Can Do

In summary :

1. *Praise gets our focus off ourselves and back on God.* In our often "selfie" focused world, we need this constant reminder - life is not all about us. We may know that in our heads, but yet our hearts think differently so often. We're prone to selfishness, He desires our eyes be set firmly on Him, because that's where our true hope is found. He is worthy of our praise, no matter what we face from day to day.

"Praise him for his mighty deeds; praise him according to his excellent greatness!" Psa. 150:2

"And my tongue shall speak of your righteousness and of your praise all the day long." Psa. 35:28

2.   *Praise brings us to a place of humility.*   We remember our dependency on God, as we acknowledge our need for Him. As we praise Him as Creator and King of this world, we admit and recognize that we're not in control, but He is. He is above all.

"Let us come into his presence with thanksgiving; let us make a joyful noise to him with songs of praise! For the Lord is a great God, and a great King above all gods." Psa. 95:2-3

"I will give you thanks in the great congregation: I will praise you among much people." Psa. 35:18

3. *Praise makes the enemy flee.* It pushes back the darkness the surrounds, and blocks the attacks and hissing lies over us. Evil will not stick around if we're praising our God, who will fight our battles for us. In the

story of Jehoshaphat, we see God miraculously defeat the enemy, because of the people's obedience to praise Him.

"As they began to sing and praise, the Lord set ambushes against the men of Ammon and Moab and Mount Seir who were invading Judah, and they were defeated" 2 Chron. 20:22

4. *Praise leaves no room for complaining and negativity.* Sometimes even within our prayers, we can tend to complain about our problems. God knows our hearts. And He cares about all that concerns us. But through praise, we're focused on Him, no longer allowing too much attention to be centered around the struggles. We're reminded of what He has already done in our lives. We're reminded that He knows what concerns us, and is capable of taking care of all that burdens us.

"Bless the Lord, O my soul, and forget not all his benefits, who forgives all your iniquity, who heals all your diseases, who redeems your life from the pit, who crowns you with steadfast love and mercy." Psa. 103:2-4

"By him therefore let us offer the sacrifice of praise to God continually, that is, the fruit of our lips giving thanks to his name." Heb. 13:15

5. *Praise makes room for God's blessings over our lives.* He will not hold back His goodness, praise opens the gateway of blessing as we come into the Presence of our King.

"Enter his gates with thanksgiving, and his courts with praise! Give thanks to him; bless his name!" Psa. 100:4

"Blessed be the God and Father of our Lord Jesus Christ, who has blessed us with all spiritual blessings in heavenly places in Christ:" Eph. 1:3

6. *Praise invites His presence.* God dwells close to us when we praise Him. He lives there. He looks for it.

"He inhabits the praises of His people." Psa. 22:3

"But you are a chosen generation, a royal priesthood, an holy nation, a peculiar people; that you should show forth the praises of him who has called you out of darkness into his marvelous light;" 1 Pet. 2:9

7. *Our spirits are refreshed and renewed in His presence.* We're strengthened by His peace and refueled by His joy. Through a heart of praise, we realize that God doesn't just change our situations and work through our problems, He changes our hearts.

"In His presence, there is fullness of joy." Psa. 16:11

"Because your love is better than life, my lips will glorify you. I will praise you as long as I live, and in your name I will lift up my hands." Psa. 63:3-4

8. *It paves the way for God's power to be displayed, miracles happen.* People's lives are affected and changed. God shakes things up through praise. As Paul and Silas sat in prison, shackled, and chained, they kept right on praising God. And God sent an earthquake that shook the cells and broke the chains.

The jailer and all his family came to know Christ that very night.

"We have a choice every day in this life. To live absorbed in worry and stress, on the fast track of busy, focused only on what surrounds us, tuned into the roar of the world.

Or, we can ask God to help us take our eyes off all that may be swirling around, our problems and mess, or the voices of others. And we can look up...to Him, the One who holds it all together, and who holds us in his hands.

God desires our whole heart. He waits for us to return. He longs for us to know the power of His presence over our lives. He desires to bless us more than we could imagine. His Spirit urges us onward, calling us closer.

May He help us to look up...open our mouths...and sing praises unto him.It is our obligation to praise, yet praising brings great benefits to us.This is the nature of the love of God upon us!

What is WORSHIP?

Worship is closely associated with praise and sometimes the two words are used interchangeably. Worship is described as REVERENCE, veneration, adoration, glorification, glory, exaltation; devotion, praise, thanksgiving, homage, honor. We can see from this analysis that the majority of instances (99 of 118) of worship in the KJV Old Testament are translations of the word **shachah (שחה).** It's the feeling or expression of reverence and adoration for a deity

In other spheres its defined as:

• the acts or rites that make up a formal expression of reverence for a deity; a religious ceremony or ceremonies.

• adoration or devotion comparable to religious homage, shown toward a person or principle

. show reverence and adoration for (a deity); honor with religious rites

• treat (someone or something) with the reverence and adoration appropriate to a deity

These are very broad meanings. A "feeling" or "expression" allows almost anything to be called worship if the one feeling or expressing intends it to be worship. This situation is not unlike the meaning of art, for which the most general meaning might be "the self-expression of the individual artist who creates it." Is there some overlap between the contemporary understandings of worship and art? Whereas art would be the expression or application of human creative skill and imagination... producing works to be appreciated primarily for their beauty or emotional power

Worship is More than Music

We don't just worship through music. Worship is much more than that. Worship should be our entire life. As worship leaders then, we're not just leading them in song but directing their daily lives.

But this is not enough. Worship "in truth" connects the heart or spirit of worship with the truth about God and his work of redemption as revealed in the person of Jesus Christ and the Scriptures. David understood the importance of worshiping in truth and the necessary linkage between "truth" and the Word of God when he wrote, "Teach me your way, O Lord, and I will walk in your truth; give me an undivided heart, that I may fear [i.e., worship] your name" (Psalm 86:11 ; cf. Psalm 145:18). Here both the Old and New Covenants agree! The true worship of God is essentially internal, a matter of the heart and spirit rooted in the knowledge of and obedience to the revealed Word of God.

Is Praise different from Worship?

Now, let us review a dictionary definition of the words worship and praise. The New Illustrated Webster's Dictionary states that worship is "The act or feeling of adoration or homage; the paying of religious reverence, as in prayer, praise, etc." It can also be "The act or feeling of deference, respect, or honor toward virtue, power, or the like." This then means for example, all that you do in church like giving, bible study, testimonies, preaching....is part of worship, including the Praising in song!

Praise, as a verb, means "To express approval and commendation of; applaud, eulogize and to express adoration of; glorify (God, etc)." As a noun, the word means "Thanksgiving for blessings conferred; laudation to God; worship expressed in song. The object, ground, reason, or subject of praise."

By comparing the two definitions, we can first see that praise is part of our worship of Almighty God. We express our approval, thankfulness, and respect for Almighty God by offering praises to Him. This kind of thankfulness then becomes part of our worship of the Great God. In such an act, we show our love through obeying His commandments, living the way of life He has revealed through His written word, the Bible, communicating with Him in prayer, meeting and fellowshipping with other believers, and in offering thanks to Him.

We reviewed Strong's Concordance of the Bible definitions in the Hebrew and Greek for both words. They are similar to what we found in Webster's. Worship means to prostrate oneself before God, bow down, humbly beseech, and do obeisance or reverence. In worship, we demonstrate that compared to God, we are as nothing. Praise means to revere (with extended hands), laudation.

Here are a few examples of the Biblical use of the words worship and praise.

All the ends of the world shall remember and turn to the Lord, and all the families of the nations shall worship before You (Psalm 22:27).

My praise shall be of You in the great assembly . . . (Psalms 22:25)

Give unto the Lord the glory due to His name; Worship the Lord in the beauty of holiness. (Psalm 29:2)

Praise ye the LORD. Praise God in his sanctuary: praise him in the firmament of his power (Psalm 150:1).

Now I, John, saw and heard these things. And when I heard and saw, I fell down to worship before the feet of the angel who showed me these things (Revelation 22:8).

Then a voice came from the throne, saying, 'Praise our God, all you His servants and those who fear Him, both

And looking at both these terms, we may be dismiss the notion that associates Praise with fast tempo songs and Worship with slow tempo songs. You can have Praise songs that are slow and Worship songs that are fast. **PRAISE OR WORSHIP HAS NOTHING TO DO WITH THE SPEED/TEMPO OF A SONG!**

I often say to people **everyone can sing**. What we call discord is when somebody just decides to join you in your song and there's no more harmony in voices. Otherwise if you are doing it alone it's a musically correct line hahaha. **Let no one stop you from PRAISING AND WORSHIPPING HIM!**

CHAPTER 4

BECOMING A RECORDING ARTIST

Well, perhaps the most common question any young, aspiring musician asks is, "What is the first thing I should do to get started as a singer/musician?"

In this case what most people will be referring to is the question of becoming a recording artist. When you sing at home, in the school choir or in the church Praise team you are already singing...meaning you are a singer! However there's a difference between just singing on these platforms, and deciding to go ahead and record, putting your voice on media where others can play and listen to you even in your absence, thus BECOMING A **RECORDING ARTIST**!

The problem with this common question is that there is no "one size fits all" answer. There are so many things that can inform the next steps in your music career, including your personal goals and genre of music.

For some, singing is a natural talent, a gifting, while others just have great passion for it. Sometimes some have both the gifting and the passion. Everyone can literary sing, but some will go all the way to record their music just to let others listen. Usually we associate this step forward with people who are gifted in singing. Others will record because they have the passion and the resources to do so

In yesteryears across the world it would take the very gifted to get recording contracts with record companies. The recording studios were few, meaning if you were not gifted enough you would also never record nomatter how much passion you heard. I am in a number of gospel artists groups and most artists always sentiment that this be the norm always, so as to screen against fly by night chancers from the industry.

Up until recently, the record companies would scrutinize the talent in you to make sure they can have value for their money by investing in your recording. One would need to record a demo song or songs which would be listened to before a decision is made on whether to record you or not. Anything that would not make business sense would never be accepted. This saw a number of people who thought they could try it out in music being turned away if they weren't good enough for the company. Some eventually gave up after trying so many times, others kept trying until they were eventually accepted. This business sense of things did not spare the gospel artists who would just want so record and "spread the gospel of Jesus Christ across the nations....while....of course making a few cents" out of their gifting. Most of these record labels have closed down especially in this part of Africa where I'm writing from. These labels would sign artists to their stables, then does all the donkey-work including recording, production, marketing, distribution and even organising of shows and concerts. All the artist needed to bring onboard was the talent, the voice, and the rest would be done for them.

However these days anyone can record their music as long as they have enough resources to do so. This has been necessitated by the proliferation of recording studios, some even in backyards of houses. With the advent of technology one can even turn a kitchen into an overnight studio and record a song that can go on to be a hit on radio stations. More recording facilities now means more recording chances, shifting the competition zone from the recording studios to the radio and television stations as more music is now being produced

However in this case, I will look at a number of factors that one has to consider and be aware of from a professional perspective. I will not dwell much on matters that have to do with what used to be, but the present going forward. Yes there are still major international record companies around the world, but most of them now focus on the marketing and distribution aspect of things, the recording part is mainly done independently now. Some even go ahead and independently market and distribute their music, the advent of technology now allows for that. This means one can go ahead and pursue an independent music career, bypassing major record labels.

Perhaps let's look at this in detail, considering this becomes more of the initial decisions one has to make in entering the recording industry.

Do not delve into something because others are doing it. Have a clear call and passion for what you will do. Plan, research, and then research and plan, do not bump into things. Before you even book for studio hours to record anything, have a clear roadmap .Some of these questions might help you :

What kind of an artist will I be, Independent (Indie) or under a label?

What type of gospel music would I like to sing and what sort of instrumentation will I use for the kind of voice that I have?

What funding is needed to complete, say a single or an album? Where will I get the funding?

Will I start with a single or an album, what sort of songs will I put there?

Will I use my own band? Will I use session musicians? Where do I get them and do I have funding for them too?

After recording how will I market, promote or even sell the product?

Take a look at the following, for example:

Major Record Label vs. Independent Music Career

Perhaps the easiest thing to consider first, and something that can offer a bit of a roadmap, is whether you envision an independent music career, or if you see yourself settling into the major label world.

An independent music career can include a do-it-yourself approach, or you can connect with music businesses and labels working at the independent level. Which is right for you depends on a few different factors.

First is a matter of simple preference. Some musicians are fiercely independent and want to do it all, while others want to focus solely on their music.

Genre choice also matters, particularly if you're interested in breaking into a major-label-dominated world like pop music. Sometimes your brand of music will dictate how you need to approach your career.

Make a Plan (how do you wish to record and release your music?)

Identifying your industry path will help guide the most important next step: Making a plan.

The indie route may see you producing and releasing your own music, and either shopping it to indie labels yourself or with the help of a manager.

Entry to a major label most often requires the facilitation of a manager or a lawyer to shop your music to the labels on your behalf. But how do you attract the attention of a manager or attorney?

Playing live provides exposure to the industry and to fans, and every show brings you one step closer to winning over a manager or winning over a fan base to attract the attention of managers, labels, booking agents and others within the industry. As your base grows, demos become the next clear step.

A lot of intangibles may cloud the process of developing a music career, but persistence and dedication are key. Define your goals, make your plan, then start playing live. Setting these wheels in motion will set everything else off. You'll learn how best to react to the unique opportunities they generate for you as a growing artist.

It is getting easier by the day to release your own music and build a music career without the backing of a label. That's an exciting thing for musicians, and for a lot of people, it's the best choice. On the other hand, there's a tendency for the Do-It-Yourself route to be romanticized.

In reality, like any other kind release, the choice to self-release your music comes with pros and cons (just like a major label deal and an indie label deal). Before you decide to self-release your album, don't forget to weigh up these factors.

Advantages of Self-Releasing an Album

You Keep Your Rights: Forget worrying about confusing contracts, expensive lawyers, and accidentally signing over your music, your vision, and perhaps your first born child to some record label for life. You decide how your music is used when it is used, and how much people have to pay to use it, end of story.

You Keep the Cash: Ever marvel at the way that some extremely successful musicians are seemingly flat broke? Sure, sometimes they're in that position because they bought things like, say, gold plated gates, but often they're in the position because they're last on the list to be paid. Every person that comes in to help with your career gets a cut, but when you're doing it yourself, you get to eat the whole pie.

You Make It (Or Don't) On Your Own Terms: Even the most laid back and artist-friendly independent label is bound to have a few limitations in mind when it comes to projects they're willing to work on with you, and major labels can be extremely demanding. Some labels may want to send you back to the studio when you decide to change musical directions, or they may demand you adopt a "look" for marketing purposes. There are lots of ways you can clash creatively with a label, and depending on what kind of deal you have, sometimes the label will win. When you're the one putting out the music, you release the music you want, and only the music you want, when you want to release it. The marketing, the touring, and all of the decision will be made by you, so there will be none of the typical conflicts.

Advantages of Record Deals

They foot the Bill: One of the main reasons many people want a record deal is so there is some money behind their release. A major label deal may bring a nice advance, and even a small indie label is going to pick up many of the costs associated with releasing a record, like PR and pressing. If you release it yourself, the financial burden will be yours alone, and that can be limiting when it comes to accomplishing everything you want to get done. It could also mean you will be facing a mountain of debt if you don't sell as much as you anticipate. Also, labels will have established relationships with manufacturers and PR companies that often translate into credit agreements and reduced rates, since the labels throw a lot of business their way. When you're establishing yourself, you may be asked to pay upfront for your orders, and you can expect to pay full price.

They have the Contacts: Labels will have a stack of contacts in place that help them promote their releases—media, promoters, agents, and so on. If you're new to the music biz, you'll have to build your little black book from scratch. Of course, everyone has to start somewhere, and if you keep plugging away at self-releasing your music, you'll have your network of connections soon enough. Don't underestimate the time this can take, though. Not having these contacts in place from the outset will make your job a little harder.

They have experience: If you don't have much music industry experience to speak of, you'll face a learning curve when you start putting your music out there. There are a lot of different parts to manage and tend to. It will take some time to figure out what works —and what doesn't—for you. It can be an expensive lesson.

You save your time: Depending on your goals for your music, promoting a record can be extremely time-consuming. Arranging press, keeping track of sales, promoting the album, and booking shows are all a full-time job. When you're doing all of this work, you're not concentrating on your music. So, it's easy to find yourself in the position where you've made some good headway with the promotion of your first release, but you don't have anything fresh to follow up with because you've been consumed with the business side of things.

So there you go, these are the options you can look at and make your own decision based on what you desire and what you are capable of doing. Sometimes you also need to sit down with a few experts or experienced artists who can advise you accordingly. If you rush into something without putting much thought into it, you may end up hating the industry

BAND MANAGERS

This is another area which is not clear with a lot of musicians. Don't just appoint someone your band or artist manager without understanding what their role will be in your set up. Don't do it also because you have seen others doing it. Finding an artist manager is not the hard part - it's finding a good band manager that can be the real challenge. A lot of artists mistake a sponsor for a manager, band management is different from band sponsorship! It doesn't follow, that if somebody has the money then they can manage your band or you as an artist. Your manager needs to be someone who will have time to MANAGE the operations of the band or the artist.

How do you find a music manager? Here's what you need to know.

Decide If You Need One Right Now

Before you pass go, ask yourself this question - do you really need a manager right now? A good manager can be a vital part of your music career, but they don't come for free. When you're just getting started, management may not be the best use of your cash. Before you go manager hunting, make sure you understand what they do and why you might need one. These articles will help:

Enlisting Your Friends

What do you need a manager to do for you? If you are looking for someone who can help you book shows, send out some demos for you, set up some digital distribution and so forth - in other words, if you're at the stage of establishing yourself - then you may already know your manager. Look around your circle of friends. Is there someone who knows something about the music biz, who is organized and who loves your music?

Bingo! The downside here is that this person may need to learn as they go, but the upside is that you'll have an enthusiastic manager working cheap - not a bad deal. However just be careful professional decisions may be overruled by friendship desires!

Gather Recommendations

A manager has an extraordinary amount of influence over your career, so this is not an appointment you want to take lightly. If you don't know anyone who can serve as a manager or if you are past the point where you can work with a manager who learns with you, then ask around for referrals to good managers. Ask fellow musicians, do some research to see who manages your favourite acts, ask promoters and bookers when you do your shows and so on. If you are at the point where you need a professional manager, then you are at the point where you know people who can make these recommendations.

Getting a manager interested in working with you is much like approaching a label, agent or promoter. Be ready to provide your management prospects with some of this information:

Idea about the kind of music you make

How far along you've come in your career on your own.

Music samples – what you can do

Biography

Press clippings, if you have any

Your vision for the present and the future

After settling for someone,

Sign a Contract

For your sake and for the sake of the manager, you should never enter into any sort of management deal without a contract. If you're working with a friend and you don't have the money for a lawyer, it's ok to work on a contract together that makes everyone happy. If you're working with a manager with more experience and they hand you a complex contract, get legal advice.

Never, ever, ever sign a contract you don't understand, and never, ever, ever work with a manager without a contract.

It is important to have the same sort of music industry philosophy as your manager. If your manager is more experienced in the business than you, then you will be able to learn a lot from them. However, if, for instance, you're seeking chart music stardom and they're committed to the indie music scene, or vice versa, then the relationship is not going to work for either of you.

A manager is almost like a member of your band - the best management relationships click on the professional AND personal level. Need help figuring out if you and your potential manager see eye to eye?

SOME KEY DUTIES OF A BAND/ARTIST MANAGER

1. Attract the interest of labels

Working with a record label isn't right for everybody, but as of now, it's still the industry standard, and many artists see it as a big step in building their career. Your manager should work on making sure record labels notice you .You should focus on creating great music, and your manager should be the one making sure it's being heard by decision-makers.

2. Help you fight for a better deal

Once you have the interest of a record label, your manager is also the one who ultimately needs to make sure you aren't being taken advantage of.

3. Manage your schedule

You might not be insanely busy (yet), but hopefully you have a lot going on. Your calendar should be pretty much filled with meetings, performances, meet and greets, interviews, and the like, and if it's not, you need to get on finding some additional ways to get out there and work. It's good to keep a personal calendar, but your manager is the one who should be making sure that you are where you need to be at almost all times.

4. Get you a publishing deal

Selling albums and singles is still important these days, but the money coming in from those purchases is dwindling year after year. Because of that, things like healthy publishing deals are becoming increasingly important. Your manager should not only make sure that you have a partnership with a well-known, active publishing company, but that it's good for you,

5. Secure endorsements, syncs, etc.

Working with brands is a great way to make some cash in today's music industry, and every artist should be looking for a partnership. Whether it be playing at a branded event at SXSW or inserting your tunes into a commercial, there's a lot of money in this space, and it's your manager's job to find you opportunities.

6. Talk you up to everybody in the industry

This item might sound a bit vague, but it's vital. Your manager shouldn't just be someone who works for you from nine to five and then goes home and thinks about anything but you. It should be a person who's on all the time, and who can't wait to help the world discover your music. This person should bring you up in almost every conversation, no matter who he or she is talking to. Whether it be to someone at a record label, the booking person for a venue or a festival, or even just some intern at an unrelated music company, you want your manager bragging about you and what you have coming up. Word of mouth is very important in the music industry, and the more people in the business hear your name, the more intrigued they will be to check you out and possibly work with you.

YOUR SONG

Now that the management and planning issues would have been dealt with, it may be time to look at what you are going to record perse. Song writing is also a talent on its own. Not all great singers are great song writers. Very few are able to write good songs and sing them well. Its always good to identify what you are gifted in. In gospel music we are a family, under the banner of Jesus Christ. God is love and working together is part of that belief system. In areas where you are not very strong, always ask others for assistance. If you have a beautiful voice but can't write songs, than ask others to write for you. The trend with most internationally famous artists is that they provide the voice, some\body provides the words, yet another provides the melody and arrangement. The results are often Mega hit songs year after year for such artists. This is one advantage of artists who always network and you can start on that kind of footing as well. As an artist don't keep yourself in a cocoon, reach out and make connections and contacts, you will need them as you grow or develop your talent.

SOME QUALITIES OF A GOOD SONG

These are some, but not limited to. When you go on to record your song you can test it against some of these qualities before publishing it.

Unique Element: Anything that makes the song stand out so that it's considered as one of a kind. These days you will find easy sing-alongs leaving "hangovers" in people's heads, easily becoming hits. These are songs with catchy hooks easily remembered.

It Isn't Defined by a Genre: Though genres do help us in choosing the songs we know we have taste in, but when genres dictate the texture of songs itself, it becomes boringly monotonous and pretty predictable. It loses its surprise element and doesn't help us in broadening in our perspective of music itself. Genres are made for convenience in categorizing music but they don't define music itself

Meaningful Lyrics: Hits that turn into classics often have meaningful words that people can relate to. Songs with lyrics that are exciting but meaningless often become short lived hits, the bubblegum type which looses tastes the more it's chewed

Complex Beats In Perfect Sync With Each Other: If you have decided to use complex beats, ensure they perfectly sync, and when you do live shows try as much as possible to reproduce such complexities to make your sound unique

Vocals in sync with the Music: After finishing your recording always take time to listen to the mix before mastering. Ensure the vocals are syncing with the music

Perfect Intro: A rather bland intro of a really great song doesn't make the song really great. An intro is the most important piece of music just as the outro, and the quality of it most either makes or breaks the song. When people sample songs, even Djs that you give your music to, they won't have time to listen to the whole track if the into is a cliché or too ordinary.

Awesome Aural Environment: The general nature of the song right from its sound output, words, and instruments gives its general feel. Good songs often have feels that make you want to play them over and over again

Surprising Use of Musical Elements: Often good songs have instruments that are not predictable. A void copying progressions and sounds from other artists' songs and try to be as original with your instrumentation, as possible.

Powerful Vocals: You may have a well written song , beautiful voice but yet fail to stamp your authority on your song. This is your song which people will listen to for many years to come, your voice needs to be confident .Don't rush, it over and over until you get it right!

With all these key areas and decisions having been made, you may now go ahead to book and record your song or album. The next two areas are choosing the right studio and choosing the right producer. This is your own personal decision, but the following tips may help you.

THE RECORDING PROCESS

In this modern age you will discover that most of the people we call "producers" are doing both engineering and production tasks in one studio, unlike previously where such roles were separated

When you get into the studio to get your song recorded, you will discover most studios are now digitalised. Most studios have in-house producers, but you can always work with a producer of your choice. These days you discover an error that we shall touch on in later chapters where an artist engages a producer who will play all instruments and do all the engineering work, plus song arrangement as well some of the backing vocals too! If you want to sound different, invest in having your own musicians/instrumentalists who have rehearsed with you, take those into the studio and free the producer/engineer to focus on doing his best with what you have brought

Ensure you get a producer who understands the type of music that you want to record. The fact that you are a gospel singer does not mean you will sing like all the others. Therefore you mistakenly think a producer who works with many gospel artists automatically knows how to get the best out of you. In the previous chapter we looked at gospel music being the message and not the beat or instrumentation. Always find a producer who is able to capture the kind of instrumentation you desire for your song. There s no harm of offence in requesting to listen to sample songs that producer has done before and check if that's the kind you are looking for. Don't go to a studio because that's where your friend records! Do your research wisely. The following is what usually happens in the studio:

1. Recording of guide instruments

2. Capturing of vocals

3. Filling in of the rest of the instruments

4. Mixing of the song

5. Mastering

Mixing and mastering music are two separate but equally important parts in the audio production process. Basically, mixing is the step before mastering that involves adjusting and combining individual tracks together to form a stereo audio file after mixdown. The stereo file is then mastered, which ensures that the various songs are clearly polished and form a cohesive whole on an album. Audio mastering engineers often offer sequencing services for albums to put the songs in the desired order, label track names, as well as encode the tracks with ISRC. The mastering engineer's primary goal is to provide a high fidelity, high clarity, professional sound that can be enjoyed by listeners on any source. This defines mixing and mastering in their simplest forms

Even though you might be having a good producer, be involved in all these stages because if you leave most of this work to the producer, he or she may end up reproducing what they did for another artist previously. Remember they work with many artists, so for your song to be unique you would rather work with them and ensure its coming out in a way both you and the producer feel will make it extra-ordinary. Don't rush things too, take your time.

Personally after mixing, I request to take the mix home, listen to it over and over and take note of any changes i may need to make before take the mix back to the producer/engineer to make final adjustments even of lyrics. Listening to the mix away from the studio gives me the space and environment that is conducive to make such adjustments. In the process sometimes I may do a couple of consultations too. This is what makes me take a number of days or weeks to do just one song, yet I still see artists taking less than 2 hours in studio, this is a recipe for compromising on quality.

Most artists ignore the last stage of song production which is mastering. Not all recording studios or producers can master, always check with your producer if they have such a facility. Don't just rush with your song to some audience without its proper professional finalisation otherwise you may destroy the song as will be explained in a later chapter.

Proper professional Mastering will ensure your song is given an ISRC. The **'International Standard Recording Code'** (or ISRC code) is a unique identification system for sound recordings and music video recordings. Each ISRC code identifies a specific unique recording and can be permanently encoded into a product as a kind of digital fingerprint. Wherever that song is reproduced, that code will show and will trace back the song to you. This helps a lot in royalties when the song undergoes revenue making processes in any part of the world

After your song is complete, whether as a single or as an album, the last stage before you release it is to register yourself and your works:

REGISTRATION TO RIGHTS ORGANISATIONS

It is very important to register your works with a rights organisation like ZIMURA (Zim), SAMRO (RSA) etc not only to ensure the rights to your works are legally protected but also for revenue collection from such works.

Some of the duties of such Rights Associations or Organisations are:

To create value for the creators and users of music;

To protect the intellectual property rights of writers, composers and music publishers by licensing music users;

To ensure that members whose works are broadcast and played commercially are paid their royalties from licence fees

To actively promote the value of copyright.

Amongst many other duties.

For example if you author your song and it's used by another artist in full or in part, such organisations help in resolving the disputes that may arise or in ensuring you get rewarded for your part. Even after death your family will still continue to benefit from your works

Rights Organisations protect the rights of composers and authors (music creators) both locally and internationally. They collect on your behalf licence fees from music users – television broadcasters, radio stations, in-store radio stations, pubs, clubs, retailers, restaurants and all other businesses that broadcast, use or play music.

Copyright is a set of exclusive rights granted to the original songwriter or composer. These rights ensure the author receives his or her due in the form of royalties earned from the reproduction, distribution and adaptation of his or her work.

Members who are composers and songwriters assign the rights of their musical works to such organisations to administer. They, in turn, use the assignments to license individuals and businesses that use music for business or commercial purposes. This includes shopping centres, nightclubs, television and radio broadcasters, and so on. They collect these licence fees from music users, which are paid out to members in the form of royalties during annual distribution cycles (after administration costs are deducted).This will ensure that creators are rewarded for the public use of their intellectual property.

After having done all this, you are ready now to reproduce copies and release your music to public domain. Some studios do everything, however if you go the indie way then you can look for those who specialise in production

Factors to consider in Production

Ensure you use a reputable production company that guarantees quality on all media e.g. CDs, DVDs, Flash drives etc

Remember with mass productions and sales your never know where your discs may end up. Never compromise on quality production. Ensure you also crosscheck randomly on the sound output of your final products. Don't go for cheap quality media; use reputable CD, DVD, Flash brands. Remember the cheapest will always be the most expensive as it will cost you later when people complain and return your products! You need to make a good impression and product quality compromise is a big weapon of destruction to your career.

Get impressive and striking quality pictures done by professional photo studios for your sleeves and covers, These may be expensive, but one well-done pic is worth it, it tells a big story about the content of your album or single, the impression it gives may either turn a person away from sampling your song or may attract them to want to listen. MANY ARTISTS DO NOT TAKE THEIR BRANDING SERIOUSLY (We will look at this in detail later)

Get a reputable designer to do your artwork as well.

Importance of good pictures and good artwork

According to Ian Inglis, photography and sleeve (or album) design are two areas of the visual arts that have been especially important to popular music's development. Photographs add additional meaning to music, both in images of performers themselves and through other types of photographs used in record sleeves and advertising. Photographic images of musicians usually take one of two forms:

Portraiture taken in a studio or other location

Live shots which aim to capture the excitement and spirit of a particular performance.

Both have been crucial in the process of image creation and in providing a star image for popular music performers. When printed in magazines and newspapers or used in cover art for records, a well taken shot can help to make a star. These types of image are also important in placing popular music acts in terms of both social context and musical style. The choice of location, style of dress, lighting and composition all help to locate an artist within a pre-existing set of visual, artistic and social associations. Often the conventions used in photographing particular types of musicians can lead to a kind of visual language that can be used and reused. So strong are these types of visual signs that we can often garner a good idea of what a particular musical act will sound like from photographs alone.

Record sleeves have a basic practical purpose: to provide packaging to encase sound carriers such as LPs and CDs. Such packaging normally includes a front cover that identifies the artist (or artists) and title of the recording alongside some form of photographic or graphic design. Over time this practical necessity has become an area for artistic expression but even the best album covers are more than just artwork. They also say something about the music. In a variety of ways the cover of an album aims to provide listeners with an initial visual context for the act or music contained on the recording. Visual representation included on record sleeves can serve to highlight the artist, genre, origin or mood of the music being packaged. As Ian Inglis notes, the sleeve is an accompaniment to the music and "not a superfluous thing to be discarded during the act of listening, but an integral component of the listening which assists and expands the musical experience" (2001, 84). As such, LP and CD cover art has been a central part of the marketing of recordings, not only placing them in terms of style but also in the importance placed upon recordings as artefacts, or collectable items.

Once all this is done YOU ARE READY TO GO! In the following chapter, we now look at how you will promote and market your product.

CHAPTER 5

EFFECTIVE MARKETING

PROMOTING YOUR MUSIC

Unless you have major label money behind you, the ability to self-promote your music is one of the most important skills you can have. When you don't have money to hire PR people to run media campaigns for you, it is up to you to make sure people know about the music you are making. Getting started can be a little overwhelming, however. These steps will help you start out on the right foot, to make sure all of the right people are standing up and taking notice of you.

Identify Your Goals

When you set out to promote your music, don't try to cover too much ground at once. Look at the way larger artists are promoted—they have specific campaigns that promote specific things, like a new album or a tour. Choose one thing to promote, like:

A single

A show

A website

Once you know what to promote, you will be able to make clear goals for yourself, i.e. if you want to promote your website, then your goal is to bring traffic to the site. With these goals in mind, you'll find it easier to come up with promotion ideas, and you'll be better able to judge the success of your promotions.

Target the Right Audience

With your promotional goal in mind, figure out who the right audience for your campaign is. If you have a gig coming up, then the channel to reach the right audience for your promotion is the local print publications and radio stations in the town in which your show is happening. If you have a limited edition single coming out, your primary audience is your band mailing list, plus the media. Going for the right audience is especially important if you're on a budget. Don't waste time and money letting town X knowing about an upcoming show in town Y or a folk magazine about your new hip hop album.

Have a Promo Package

Just like when you send a demo to a label, to self-promote your music, you need a good promo package. Your package should have:

A press release detailing your news

A short (one page) band bio

A CD (a demo recording is ok, or an advance copy of an upcoming release)

A package of any press coverage you have had so far—press coverage begets press coverage

Your contact information (make sure to include an email address - people may hesitate to call you)

A color photo, or a link to a site where a photo can be downloaded. The press is more likely to run a photo if they don't have to chase it.

Find Your Niche

The sad truth is, every writer, radio station, website, or fan for that matter, you are trying to reach is likely being bombarded with info from other music hopefuls. You need a reason to stand out. Try to find something that will make people more curious about you—give them a reason to want to know more. You don't have to devise a huge, calculated persona, but giving people a reason to check out your show or your CD before the others can only help.

Branding

Get your name out there. Make up some stickers, badges, posters, or anything else you can think of that include your band's name. Then, leave the stuff anywhere you can. Pass them out at churches around you, leave them at shop and supermarket counters, at hair salons etc—go for it. Soon, your name will be familiar to people even if they don't know why, and when they see your name in the paper advertising an upcoming show, they'll think "hey...I know that name, I wonder what that's all about.."

Keep Track of Your Contacts

As you go through all of these steps, chances are that you are going to pick up a lot of new contacts along the way. Some of these contacts will be industry people and some will be fans. Never lose track of a contact. Keep a database on your computer for the industry people you have met and another database of fan contacts. These databases should be your first port of call for your next promotional campaign - and these databases should always be growing. Don't write anyone off, even if you don't get much feedback from them. We shall look at this again under social media marketing. Never lose contact of anyone who comments or posts about how they love your music. In the arts industry these are treated as "gold", one fan is a huge asset, respond to and treat them well

You never know who is going to give you the break you need.

Know When to Act Small

This step ties in with targeting the right audience and identifying your goals - you can save a lot of time spinning your wheels by keeping the small stuff small. While it's always useful to keep other people up to date with what's happening in your career. When you're getting started, the easiest place to start a buzz is your local area.

Build up the small stuff to get to the bigger stuff.

But Know When to Act Large

Sometimes, a larger campaign really is in order. Go full speed ahead when you have something big brewing, like:

A new album

A tour

An important piece of news, like an award or a new record deal

This kind of news warrants contacting both the media and people you want to work with, like labels, agents, managers and so on.

GET PUBLICITY FOR THE RIGHT REASONS

Gospel music is associated with Christianity and therefore aligned with a certain type of life and moral conduct. Usually people tend to dissociate themselves from Gospel artists who court controversy. In many countries once your way of life begins to be contrary to what you are singing, you face resentment and shinning form your followers. Artists doing other kinds of music can actually gain popularity over controversy, but that's a no go area for Gospel artists! Make sure you get noticed for the right reasons. Generally you certainly will get some attention for bad, unprofessional behaviour, but the problem is that your music won't be what everyone is talking about - and isn't that what you really want to be recognized for? Don't do yourself the disservice of self-promoting a bad rep for yourself. Make sure you get noticed for your talent instead. Also, don't be fake! If you're not sure what your niche is yet, don't push it.

Stay true to yourself and your music.

Grow your Database

In addition to keeping tracks of the contacts you have, don't be afraid to help your database grow by adding some "dream" contacts to your list. Is there an agent you want to take notice of you? Then include them on your press release mailing list or promo mailing list when you have big news to share. Let them know you're still working and still building your career—pretty soon, they may be knocking on your door.

Take a Deep Breath

For many people, the idea of self-promoting their music to their fans is easy, but the idea of calling up the press is downright terrifying. Relax. Here's the truth—some people you call will be nice, some people won't be. Some people will never return your calls or emails. Some will. You shouldn't take any of it personally. You definitely shouldn't be afraid to try. Covering bands is the job of the music media - they expect to hear from you. Don't be discouraged by someone who is rude, or someone who is polite, but still says "no".

Don't write them off, either. Next time, you may hear "yes."

No matter which field you choose in life, marketing has become an integral part of every field. Whether you cook food, paint or make music marketing is something you should keep yourself updated about. If you're a new coming musician, the first thing that you will need is to increase your fan base. You need to make sure that you can woo the hearts of those who take your music to another level.

Here are some marketing techniques to promote your music in this era:

Practice makes perfect

Whether it's 2018 or 2050, you can never undermine the importance of practice. Being involved in shows what will make your music better, and it will also develop an audience that experiences your music first hand. Although it isn't anything new it goes a long way. You should try to open for other singers this will give you access to a larger audience that are fans of your genre and playing in front of such an audience is sure to create new fans.

Use the power of social media

As the days pass by, social media has become an integral part of our days. Everyone is on social media regardless of the place or the time. You should use this to your advantage. You should post snippets of your music on Snapchat, use live videos to show how the process takes place such as songwriting sessions, jamming sessions so people can relate to you on a personal level. You can use Twitter to share updates and Facebook to share the stories behind every song.

Every serious artist should have at least:

Email address

Facebook page (not profile only)

Twitter account

Instagram account

Snapchat account

Develop at least a whatsapp group for your interaction with fans. Most of the posts that I see on musicians groups are meant for your personal fans groups. In this day of technology that's the way to go, technology brings us closer to our fans than ever before. The days of fliers and posters all over town when advertising shows and events are becoming a thing of the past. Even environmentalists and local authorities are discouraging such.....the alternative is social media

Now , when you release new stuff and you want people to buy or share your social media groups are your best platform .When u want people to vote for your music in different charts and Awards spheres, this is the best platform. People nowadays spend much time on their phones and a heavy social media presence by an artist ensures great interactive results. This is where a relationship and stronger bond is cultivated between the musician and their fans

Fans love to see their artist...your adventures, trips, programs etc...

Remember to go back to the previous pages, in this book, on how to grow this database of fans on social media. One other platform that I will keep emphasising on is radio interviews where you are allowed to give fans your social media contacts and platforms. Never under-utilise that kind of a platform! Whenever the fans come through after such sessions, I usually get those that help us with our social media, to capture as much detail as they can especially the names and towns or areas where those fans are based. This helps a lot when you then go to such areas for shows, concerts etc..You can always alert those in the area. Some of them are even willing to help in the marketing of events in their areas

If you do your social media work correctly u reap the results

Create a professional website

While social media will play an active role in enhancing your social media presence and awareness about your music, one thing you must have is a professional website along with your updated music profile. While fans may have a greater presence on social media, music companies like professionalism and a professional website give an impression that you are serious about your music and want to take it to the next level. Some even sell their music on those websites as well

Become an all-rounder

The number of musicians is increasing with the increase in pop culture and music in general. The number of students pursuing music as a career is rising each year. You should think about what percentage makes it into the spotlight, only a handful. Nowadays music is more than just music; you have videos and performances. You should be a fantastic performer and an amazing singer.

Collabos and giveaways

Another Major trend nowadays is collaboration songs and videos. If you're an aspiring music artist, find other people and make collaborative music. This usually helps new artists gain confidence when they collaborate with older artists in the industry. Sometimes people would give the song attention because of a popular name they know who is featured on that song, in the process getting to know the newer artist better. In Collabos, one must just be careful not to let the older artist steal the limelight or sing more lines on the song because eventually it will be identified as a song by the already established artist (what we call name drowning!)

You can also arrange for giveaways, who doesn't like free stuff and giveaways are an excellent incentive to use to promote music. It might appear a loss because you are giving for free, but it's an investment that gives you bigger results later

Having said this, I know new artists often focus their promotional efforts heavily toward the digital space (which is understandable and should make up a major part of your promo campaigns). **However, never underestimate the power of live performance.**

CHAPTER 6

CHALLENGES IN EXECUTING THE MISSION

In this chapter I will look at some of the challenges faced by artists in general, with a bias towards gospel musicians. I will attempt to suggest possible solutions to those challenges using my own personal experiences and also some researched ideas. These solutions are not prescriptive, just a guide on things you can try in order to overcome the raised challenges.

Challenge #1: Wearing too many hats

For independent musicians, you usually have no choice but to do it yourself – whether you know what you're doing or not. You end up being the singer, the co-producer, the promoter, the distributor, the marketer, the doorman......Action has to happen from within, because it's not coming from anywhere else.So says Michael Prentky of Boston-based Mozambican group Kina Zoré. "I took it upon myself to fill the gap. It took me a long time to learn the protocol, the etiquette, the language, the formality (or lack thereof), and, most importantly, the stick-to-it-iveness to get shows."

Suggested Solution:

Find ways to delegate. "Kina Zoré is still learning about how to best balance all of these things," Prentky explains. "We definitely have a more established protocol now, but are very much in the midst of figuring out how to choose where and when to play which shows, and how to best promote them. We've gotten better at dividing up tasks – who does social media, who does posters, who goes to concerts to pass out handbills, etc. – just learning what exactly to do, what works, and how to execute it as a group."

"Do it. Get help. Learn," explains Harjinder Singh from Chicago-based band Fatbook. "Don't get destroyed by the overwhelming task at hand, but conquer it. It will be hard, but things you accomplish from the ground up are super rewarding! There are so many different ways to envision that process and outcome. There's isn't one right answer, especially because the modality of this industry is in such a flux and state of opportunity at the same time."

Challenge #2: Finding reliable band members

Being a bandleader means also managing "the wild and crazy personalities, lives, and schedules of your musicians – and still having your band by the end of the day. Sometimes members will leave you at a crucial time, some even without communicating. Using session members also backfires on days when they get double booked

Suggested Solution:

Communication. "People are dynamic, moving forces. Open communication is an ongoing need," says Singh. It is always important to have time to sit with your members one by one, listen to their problems, how they live...draw them closer, love them and make them feel loved. Sometimes when we lose those relationship qualities we also loose people from our lives. It's also good to work with people that you personally groom and grow the vision together with. Desist from the tendency of "poaching" musicians from other artists; these things always have a way of coming back to you at crucial moments!

Challenge #4: Lack of support and human resources

At times, being a artist can be so daunting. Perhaps you want to take your career to the next level, whether that means recording an album or going on tour, but you don't have the resources or the means to acquire do it.

Suggested Solutions:

Surround yourself with people you trust. It's important to make sure you're only delegating to people or organizations who truly care about your project as much as you, The entertainment industry is full of people who want to make money, but the key is to surround yourself with people who truly appreciate your creations and care as much about facilitating your success as what they tangibly gain from helping you.

Find investors. There are people who want to support your art – and you need them to support your art. Create a network for your project to get the resources it needs – make it bigger than just what you think it is. Those people are part of your project, too, whether they're the scene kid who comes to all your shows and knows all your songs, or the independently wealthy person that doesn't know anything about your music but wants to be a donor for the arts. There are so many ways for people to be a part of your art – let them join the team." Sometimes you need to come out of the closet, remove the "celebrity touch-me-not syndrome" and be open about needing help and support. People will never know what you need until you say it.

Challenge #5: Lack of Airplay

Well, this is one cry I have heard since the 90s when I started recording music. It looks like it's always been there since time immemorial. In these days and age the radio stations have increased in number but still the airplay complaint is increasing

Suggested Solution

First of all your song will never play at a station that you have never sent it to! When you are under a record label, the company can take this task and you sit back and relax, but when you are an indie like, most of the artists these days, then you have to just do it yourself. After your song has been released, ensure you visit every radio station library and submit your song in the format a and quantities required. It's important that you try and do it personally so that when you visit the station you also get a chance to meet with and create a relationship with the people who will play that music, the DJs. Let them have something to say about you when they play your song because they have met with you and you are in constant touch with them. Don't just remember a DJ because you have a new release only, create relationships and let them understand you better as an artist. ALL relationships are centred on communication. And after submitting your song make a follow-up that its now on the station playlist and ask your fans to also support it through musical request programs as well as radio chart shows

Then you also need to realise radios are not the only media that broadcast and play songs. Remember as the years go by, more and more artists are recording their songs as well unlike previous years. So cramming and jamming one radio station for play when there are more than 10 gospel albums born each day would be a mammoth task. Make use of social media and even online radio and TV stations that are now all over the world. Check the previous chapter on the issue of social media presence. These days you can easily reach thousands of direct listeners via platforms like Facebook, YouTube or even Whatsapp.

Challenge #6: Getting discouraged

I think the most discouraging part of being an artist is the fact that art is so subjective, You could write the greatest song in the world, and there would still be a percentage of people who wouldn't like it. They may not even have a reason for not liking it. No matter how thick your skin, rejection is always a tough pill to swallow. Most of the gospel artists start singing in their churches, and sometimes the very churches may be people who either discourage the rising artist, want their CDs for free or won't even attend their Concerts even when held at the very church.

Suggested Solutions:

Focus on the small, positive things. Carpenter, a renowned artist says : The thing that, without fail, gets me out of my own head, is just one single person who hears our music for the first time and actually takes the time and energy to send a tweet, post a comment on a video, or reach out via our website and tell us how much they love it. That is, in a nutshell, why I do all of this. Pulling an idea out of thin air and transforming it into something that touches even one or two people in a way that brightens their day or makes a moment in their life even a little sweeter is nothing short of amazing.

Learn from your mistakes. I think there's a quote somewhere: 'Success is born from failure.' I truly believe that," Carpenter adds. "There are valuable lessons to be learned by falling flat on your face, and the only way to capitalize on them is to pick yourself back up and keep moving forward."

Like I mentioned earlier on in this book, I personally had to wait till album number 10 to get the mass recognition. Discouragements came, but that didn't stop me from producing 9 albums for the few who kept telling me they were being blessed by my art. Keep going .Always appreciate and honour those men and women of God who give you platforms in their churches to minister. Such appreciation often develops into major relationships that can open the doors you desire. Avoid lots of complaints especially when given a platform to minister to an audience you didn't put together. APPRECIATION IS YOUR KEY

Challenge #7: The competition

Sometimes when you hear and see what others are doing, check on radio charts, you keep feeling like there is competition out there and you are not doing well enough. Also, the act of remaining competitive with peers in the industry who generally have much larger support teams around them can be a challenge. Others end up losing the purpose and mission of Gospel music and focus on doing better than so and so at whatever cost, whatever it takes. *This breeds corruption, backbiting and immorality!*

Suggested Solutions:

The most important thing to remember is as Gospel artists we are not in it to compete but to complement each other as part of the mission of Jesus Christ. We are family, our aims and p[purposes are the same. However, entering into charts, awards and other related platforms just helps us to check on our quality and whether we are giving people value. Even in spreading the Gospel, value is of importance if you are going to win attention. These platforms should be used to draw people to our chief mission as Gospel artists.

So how do I improve myself in such" competition" how do I make myself better? Take one step at a time. Start local and build your network as you go. Build connections. Never lose the opportunity to turn contacts into connections. It is all about GRACE for networking perseverance and talent. God will bless the work of your hands and where no such work is found then the blessing won't find somewhere to "land on" Keep playing music and making your art. Be true to yourself. Being unique is the best way to shine through.

Evaluate often. Be brutally honest with yourself . The number of trials and tribulations along the way will burn you, unless you're 100 percent dedicated. Some artists don't have the honesty to confront their music and realize improvements need to be made." Don't rush also to think you have already made it because you have a song that has been number one on some music chart or because your song has played on television. Continue to work hard; your only competition is **yourself**, JUST TRY TO DO BETTER THAN YOU DID LAST TIME!

Challenge #8: Demotivation and Wearing out

It's always more work than can be done. You're creating a business out of nowhere that has to be able to support the art you're creating in the first place, plus everything that goes along with that. The main challenge is having enough time and energy and entrepreneurial drive to create legitimate support. It's a monstrous challenge to have as much vigour as you need for your creative process.

Suggested Solution:

Set a time limit on your work process. Even as you work hard, you can't do everything and you can't be everywhere. Only God is omnipresent. A lot of artists end up burning out and sometimes demotivated as their resources dwindle due to lack of proper planning. They try to be everywhere and with everyone; eventually they burn out and become discouraged. Learn to say "NO" or "UNFORTUNATELY I CANT", these two may be great tablets for your body. Also allow yourself breaks. Just like you set aside the time and space for your practice and your sleep, you have to do the same for answering emails, booking tours, scheduling, and promoting.

Also, be realistic about what you can accomplish. Entering the music industry with false illusions makes failure more likely. You must be prepared to face obstacles and rejections and be persistent enough to keep trying to land a recording job no matter how many problems you run into. Delays and failed projects are not uncommon for recording artists. Creating a strong support system can help you stay strong when you hear "no".

Challenge #9: Poor Quality in Gospel Products

Many a times I have come across messages where people complain about lack of quality in Gospel music projects be they shows, concerts, worship events even audio and video recordings. Does it matter at all, or so long the Gospel gets to the people?

Suggested solutions

When God gave instructions to Noah for the building of the ark there were specific quality standards including measurements and type of wood to be used. Look at yourself, how you have been crafted, your body functions...and tell me God is not interested in quality! This also applied when he gave temple building instructions during the days of Solomon and his father David. Let's not associate this type of music with mediocrity just because "God only sees the heart" the rest don't matter! Value and quality are two great attributes that can also let people see"God was at work here". Master your craft. Simply being a good singer isn't enough because raw talent can only take you so far. Perfect your vocal delivery and artistic presentation. Listening to successful recording artists in your genre can help you pinpoint areas for exploration and improvement. See how others that have made it before you are doing things and take time to learn and improve. Let's have great and well organised Gospel Concerts out there, great musical videos, great launches too! Better I do one well polished song at a time than 2 albums a year that aren't different from each other at all. When people listen to your latest production, let there be some difference in quality and presentation.

When we run events let there be good planning and rehearsals too. Whether people have pain or not, they deserve respect. Plan your events in advance, schedule time slots for performers in advance, if there are artists coming to support send them the program and times in advance. If you are scheduled to perform at a particular time be there by that time. If you are not scheduled to perform, do not gate crush into people's programs or try to force them to include you because by doing so you are already disrupting their program. If you are late for your time slot, always have the courtesy to communicate. Remember, these are the things that seem very small but they make or break the respect that you so desire as an artist. THEY BUILD YOUR INTEGRITY. Respect is not forced but it's earned. THERE IS NO SUBSTITUTE FOR QUALITY!

Challenge #10: Rumours, Grapevine and Backbiting

This is one area which at one point affected me to an extent I felt like quitting. As you rise people will always talk, stories will always do rounds about you. This ranges from those that will circulate as mere grapevine to those that will get wide media coverage.

Suggested Solutions

As a Gospel artist, stop the habit of backbiting others in the trade. You will never make your own candle brighter by blowing out other people's candles. I have seen situations where we meet as artists, and then instead of discussing progressive issues we end up discussing other artists, especially those who are doing well in those days. *It looks like everybody has something to say on something they heard about them:*

He is divorcing his wife

She is sleeping her way to get television airplay

Her song is number one because she pays DJs

He was booked for that event because he has connections there

He sleeps with every vocalist he works with

She pays the top guys at the radio station

This being the trend, you will realise when you start doing well people will also not lack in terms of stories about you as well. From those that know "all your evil relations" to those that know "how you are bribing your way to the top". The best response to such is keeping on keeping on, doing what you know best, which is working hard. Don't respond or comment on every little story popped around about you, instead focus on doing better each time. Don't give such stories too much attention, following up on every rumour circulating will wear you down and discourage you.

Challenge #11: Piracy

Piracy has become more of a scourge especially in Africa. This is when people reproduce and market your music without permission and they take all the proceeds.

Suggested Solution

The only solution would have been to just tell people to stop selling other peoples music, but it's not that easy especially in countries with economic challenges. I personally believe a song like Ebenezer that become more like a National Anthem in Zimbabwe might have sold over a million copies by now, but unfortunately that has not been the case. With the advent of digital platforms for music sales, I believe online sales are the way forward. Government intervention would also make life easier for artists, but it is usually all talk and no action. Online selling seems to be the direction music sales are taking and the sooner we embrace and implement the sooner we will get something out of our music, over against piracy

Challenge #12 : Poor Concert attendances

Well I have deliberately decided to look at this challenge lastly and give it as much space as I can get. Live events are an integral part of any serious musician. Live performances bring the artist closer their fans. However one MEGA challenge a lot of Gospel artists complain about is poor attendance in Concerts and Shows.

In trying to address this challenge, I want to share with you the reasons raised by The Sail Inn. They are looking at this from the perspective of promoters who complain of poor attendances at events they would have organised. As you read though you may as well begin to develop your own solutions now from an artist perspective!

The bands may not be that good

Perhaps, the bands you invite to play in your aren't up to the standards. It can't be denied that a large majority of bands are simply starry-eyed and spend most of their time ruing about lost opportunities, rather than rehearsing and tightening their performances. It's important for these bands to record their rehearsals and shows, and then listen to them for corrections later. They should be encouraged to get their act together and double their rehearsal schedule.

You play the same bands too often

No music lover would come to see a band if it's playing three shows every alternate day. Customers or music lovers don't like frequenting such venues as there are just too many alternatives available in the marketplace. They've got ample options to have a good time and enjoy good music. It's recommended to schedule at least one big local show after every 4 to 6 weeks. It'll give you ample time for promoting that show and building some buzz around it.

They come across as just another event

You must turn every show into a major event! Spread them out evenly if you need to and come up with innovative themes and titles for all your shows. They should sound like fun and people should be talking about them in advance, on both online and off-line platforms.

You may not be selling enough advance tickets

It's always a good idea to sell advance tickets of a show as it encourages people to book their spot and commit to the show. Make sure that these advance tickets are much cheaper than your actual door price. If there is a possibility of getting hard tickets printed, it would do you a world of good to involve local music stores into the ticket sales process. There is an old world charm and fun in the activity of going and picking up tickets for a music show! And music enthusiasts love that! Furthermore, work hand-in-hand with the bands to promote their shows.

Bands are completely unaware of their responsibilities

Many bands believe that it is entirely the promoter's responsibility for promoting their shows. They must be reminded that there's no guarantee that people are going to come in hoards for a show just because it's listed on the event calendar of a popular venue. You, as a promoter may have too many shows on your hand to promote any one single artist or band. You can't expect even the hard-core loyalists to turn out for each and every show. Inevitably, bands will need to share the responsibility of pulling in the crowds.

Poor planning and marketing

No event can turn itself into a miracle if not properly planned, whether it's done at family level, church level, or society level. Some artists advertise their product launches live recordings and even concerts a year in advance just for planning and marketing purposes, yet others arrange theirs in a week and expect wonder crowds. Anything that is not properly planned will flop nomatter which artists are involved. Remember these days churches are also inviting the same artists to their crusades and conferences where the audiences "pay nothing" to see them. Therefore if you will bring the same artist again for a fee into the same area, then you have to plan well and make people see value in now paying for the same artist they saw "for free" last month at their church. This is what makes Gospel Shows decline in numbers, people will need to see value for their time and money, otherwise they will wait for the next church conference. FAILING TO PLAN IS PLANNING TO FAIL

Well there are so many challenges facing the Gospel music industry at the moment, I would not be able to exhaust them all. These are some of the big ones, and like I said before, these solutions are not prescriptive but just guidelines that might help. We need to continue looking at ways to overcome. IF WE KEEP PUTTING OUR HEADS TOGETHER WE CAN MAKE THINGS EASIER US AND OTHERS, UNITED WE STAND

CHAPTER 7

MAKING MONEY AS AN ARTIST

Do Gospel artists also need to make money or they are doing it for God? Well this is a question most fans ask, especially those who don't want to pay their way into shows or those who want freebies like cds and DVDs. Surprisingly the same people will pay to buy a bible, which contains the very Word of God.

Even though singing is a gift from God and given for free:

Travelling to a studio or to events isn't free

Booking the studio inst free

Production of Cds isn't free

Band Rehearsals aren't free either

Musicians playing in the band don't eat "God Bless You s"

Even travelling to sing for you at your church is not paid by "holy water" the cars need fuel or the taxis will require cash

THEREFORE EACH TIME YOU GET AN ARTIST SONG FOR FREE YOU ARE KILLING THEIR POTENTIAL TO GIVE YOU MORE MUSIC. A lot of artists that I started recording with in the 90s have already folded due to lack of money.

So the answer is YES, GOSPEL ARTISTS NEED MONEY, LOTS OF IT! Money may not be the CHIEF reason why we are singing, but MONEY HELPS US GET TO THAT CHIEF REASON AND MISSION FASTER! Just like churches need money to run their programs, so do your gospel musicians too.

Selling CDs and holding shows are not the only ways artists can use to get money.

In this chapter I will rely more on the input of David Cole and present about 18 ways in which a musician can make money.

18 Ways Musicians Can Make Money

1. **CD Sales**: If you're going to be playing live shows, having CDs on hand is still a good idea. They make great takeaway souvenirs that can easily be signed by band members.

2. **Endorsements and Brand Ambassadorial roles**: When companies and organisations use you as a brand ambassador or for their campaigns they will usually pay out something to you. It's a huge way of earning something especially when your name or brand has grown as well. They can even help you generate extra income for your next recording

3. **Digital Sales**: You should be selling digital music through your own website to make the most money, but also through online retailers. Keep in mind that online retailers take a percentage of sales (ex. iTunes takes 30%, Bandcamp takes 15%). Some digital distributors that place your music in stores like iTunes and Amazon will take a cut on top of that.

4. **Streaming**: Although per-stream payouts from streaming services tend to be small, they can add up over time. Keep in mind that these services also help new fans discover your music, and shouldn't be seen solely as an income generator.

5. **Live Shows**: Money made from live shows can vary greatly, but it's still one of the best ways to earn income. Not only can you make money from selling tickets, but it's also one of the best ways to sell merchandise.

6. **Physical Merchandise**: Income from physical merchandise can depend heavily on the amount of live shows you play. If you go out on tour, be sure that you have some t-shirts, as well as smaller items like buttons and stickers that you can sell to fans after the show.

7. **Digital Merchandise**: You can also sell digital merchandise items like PDFs, videos, and images to your fans. Things like lyric books, live concerts, sheet music, exclusive photos, artwork and more.

8. **Crowdfunding**: Crowdfunding can be a great way to generate income for your music career. A well-executed crowdfunding campaign can help you raise enough money to offset the cost of producing and marketing your album.

9. **Publishing Royalties**: You should be signed up to a performing rights organization so you can collect royalties on your music. This includes public performance royalties (radio, TV, live venues), mechanical royalties (sales through retailers, streaming, etc.), and sync royalties (commercials, film, TV).

10. **Digital Royalties**: Whenever your music is played on services like SiriusXM radio, Pandora, and webcasters, they must pay royalties.

11. **Live Performance Royalties**: When performing original material, you can earn royalties from live performances. Whether you perform at restaurant or other music venue, Performance Rights Organizations (PROs) will pay royalties from those live performances.

12. **Licensing**: If you get your song placed in a film, commercial, or TV show, chances are they're going to pay you a licensing fee. These fees vary greatly, depending on the budget for the project, and how badly they want your particular song.

13. **YouTube**: On YouTube, whenever your music is used in videos that are running ads, YouTube pays a portion of that advertising money to the rights holders of the song. Digital distributors like TuneCore and CD Baby can help you collect that money, as well as Audiam.

14. **Sponsorships**: If you've built up a fan base, some companies are willing to sponsor musicians to reach those fans. Sponsorships can range from cash, to free products, services, and gear.

15. **Session Work**: Another way to make some extra money is to put yourself out there as a session musician. As a singer or instrumentalist, you could do

session work for other musical projects, or even in advertising.

16. **Songwriting/Composing**: If you're a songwriter, you could write songs for other musicians, or compose music specifically for film and television.

17. **Cover Gigs**: Playing cover gigs at restaurants, weddings, and other private events is frowned upon by some musicians. But those shows can pay really well, and allow you to get paid to play your instrument.

18. **Music Lessons**: Many musicians teach their instrument to others to help generate revenue towards their own career. This can be a nice way to supplement your income, and allows you to hone your craft at the same time.

The we go, the more of these money making methods you apply the better the chances of you generating more revenue and the longer you will stay in this music ministry. DO THE BEST YOU CAN

CHAPTER 8

AN EFFECTIVE MINISTER

MOST GOSPEL SINGERS BECOME WORSHIP LEADERS IN THEIR CHURCHES!

Finally, I would not have done justice to this book title if I don't look at the gospel singer as a minister. The gospel singer as a worship leader. Yes the singing has the business aspect, which I have tried to deal with as thoroughly as I could in the previous chapters. But it has a ministry side which we will delve into in this chapter.

An effective Gospel singer should desire to become an effective Gospel minister. Well some people are into Gospel Music for the financial rewards, for some it's a career path bringing career income, yet for others it's a ministry, a calling, to use for soul-winning purposes. You will also find a lot who combine all these purposes in one person. I will just say like Paul says in Philippians 1 : 18 .... 18 *What then? notwithstanding,* *every way, whether in pretence, or in truth, **Christ is preached**; and I therein do rejoice, yea, and will rejoice.*

There are some who may not even desire to record their music for further public consumption. These are the ones who may want t remain just as part of church Praise and Worship teams and nothing more. You will see them at the crusades but never in a studio, and all by choice.

With these factors in mind, let us then look at some qualities of effective worship leadership, which will apply to all gospel singers who seek to understand deeper things of this calling.

While today's worship leaders are expected to possess a great many abilities, spiritual or musical, there are a few, which are above styles or fads that come and go. I believe these qualities come under this category and are therefore essential for any worship leader to retain and practice consistently.

1. Prayerful Life

(Luke 5:16, Matthew 6:6)

A worship leader must be a person of prayer, setting apart at least an hour every day for silent prayer, Bible reading & reflection. Some recommended best practices are praying in the morning, choosing a place where one can be alone, memorizing at least one Bible verse during this time and turning off all sources of distraction / noise like mobile phones / music players. The journey of becoming a worship leader begins with being a worshipper and there's absolutely no substitute for daily personal prayer.

2. Listening Ear

(1 Samuel 3:10, Numbers 9:7-9)

A worship leader should be a keen listener with ears habitually open to hear and obey what the Lord says – like Samuel and Moses. Whether it's planning a set-list, organizing practice sessions, forming a team, recruiting new members or training others, it must all start with checking with God on what He wants and then doing just that.

3. Team Player

(1 Corinthians 12:15-17)

The worship leader should meet with other members regularly to pray as a team, work out/practice songs together, understand each other's strengths & limitations and move towards becoming a united ministry. The person operating the sound system or lyrics projection is as important as the drummer or lead guitarist on stage, so treating everyone with respect and working together as a team are high priority qualities. Outside ministry, he/she should also build and maintain good relationships with others.

4. Servanthood

(1 Peter 5:5, 1 Timothy 5:17)

A worship leader must be a humble servant of the church, willing to work with and for others – the pastor/preacher, people in other ministries, (intercession, mercy-works, healing, deliverance etc.). For example, if the pastor asks for a particular song to be removed from or added to a set-list, the worship leader must have an attitude of submission and comply. He/she must have a sound understanding of the vision of the local church, how each ministry is working towards it and ensure the worship ministry also plays its role accordingly.

5. Musical Skill

(1 Chronicles 25:7, 2 Chronicles 34:12)

Earlier, I mentioned there's no substitute for personal prayer. On the other hand, there's no substitute for practice either. In the books of Chronicles we read about how the Levites were skilled in music for the Lord. Similarly, the modern worship leader must also spend quality time in developing vocal or musical skill. The minimum level needed is to be able to sing on pitch and play the right chords. Even if he/she is a non-musician, learning basic concepts like key, rhythm and tempo is essential for team communication. The worship leader should also identify improvement areas in the ministry and lookout for adequate training opportunities.

6. Ministerial Competency

(Psalm 92:1)

Worship is not music, but a mediocre worship leader can reduce it to just that – a mere musical performance of songs with Christian lyrics. Here is where the quality of ministerial competence comes in. The worship leader must know how to deliver a worship set in a manner that people encounter God during the session; how scripture, prayers, music and songs tie-in together; how to minimize distractions; how to seamlessly transition from one song to the next; how to engage the congregation in participative worship; what the different worship progressions are and how they can be used; how to leverage technology in ministry and so on.

7. Pursue Excellence

(1 Corinthians 14:12, 1 Thessalonians 4:1, 1 Corinthians 9:24)

A worship leader should not be easily satisfied even when things are going well. He/she should look to the Lord with an expectant faith and wait on Him at all times to know what's next. Taking constructive feedback from others and working on any limitations identified are good practices for continual improvement. Making oneself accountable to someone (an elder or spouse or friend etc.), sharing and praying with that person regularly will help strengthen one's personal walk with Christ. The worship leader should constantly and passionately strive to "be excellent in what is good" – Romans 16:19

Change the way you see and approach rehearsals

Many choirs and praise teams don't show much enthusiasm at choir rehearsal because for many of us we're dragging ourselves there after long days at work. We're tired. And honestly, we just don't see it as much more than "rehearsal". This is absolutely a mindset/attitude issue.

Our results change dramatically when our attitude and mindset towards rehearsal changes from "rehearsal" to "preparation to minister to God's people". When you begin to see rehearsal as preparation to deliver a word from God to His people, it takes on a different meaning. The work of perfecting a song can be something you dread or something you enjoy and see as a necessary part of effective, anointed ministry. It can be one more thing you have to drag yourself to, or it can be a spiritual and emotional lift that gets you through the week. The difference lies in how you choose to see it.

Remember The Purpose!

Yet musicians can sometimes get into trouble when they don't understand their place and move out of their calling. Ezekiel 28 tells us the story of a gifted musician who had a great job. He was the anointed music minister of heaven. But he began to be dissatisfied with his portion of the "glory."

In his pride and rebellion, he attacked his leader and eventually lost everything including his job and position. His rebellion was so complete; he can never get back what he had. You've probably figured out we are talking about Lucifer, known now as Satan. Get this; **the only church split in heavenly history was caused by the music minister**.

Music ministry was never meant to stand on its own. It is not listed as one of the five-fold ministry gifts found in Ephesians 4:11 - gifts that are the foundational building blocks of the church. I believe it is found in the gifts listed in 1 Corinthians 12:28 as the five-letter word "H-E-L-P-S." When teamed with and submitted to a ministry gift, such as a pastor, music can have a powerful place in the vineyard

We see this historically in the church. Billy Graham had the great singer, George Beverly Shea, as his partner for many years in his crusades. Such a combination produced great results. A man named Barnabus accompanied the apostle Paul on his travels, and Barnabus was historically known to be a singer.

If you are a music minister, beware of rebelling against your authority - it sets you up for a fall. No leader is perfect, but if you'll serve your leader as according to God's Word, you will enjoy servitude with a purpose, and THE BLESSING THAT ACCOMPANIES SUCH SERVITUDE WILL FOLLOW YOU ALL THE DAYS OF YOUR LIFE!

CONCLUSION

After all has been said and done, we thank God if somebody has benefited from this book. It has always been my hope and desire to come up with such literature based on what I have seen and experienced in this industry even for the little time that I have been in it. This will certainly not be the last book I will write as my little contribution to this industry, I believe more and more literature will come as long as God has allowed .And this is not all that is to the Gospel Music Industry, there's more that I have left out. But I believe this information might be useful to any beginner.

Artists should remember that when you partake in singing gospel music, you are actually spreading the gospel. You are also partaking in a ministry which had a leader sometime ago, called Lucifer. However this leader was deposed and the role he used to play is now done by you! Now you can imagine how angry and jealousy he is when he sees you holding that microphone and praising your maker!

Ezekiel 28:12-13 ...the workmanship of thy tabrets and of thy pipes was prepared in thee in the day that thou wast created."

This is the main reason why you will find praise and worship leaders, choir leaders, band leaders and even artists themselves being the main targets of attacks. Not only that but most strife and despondency in many churches either starts in the music teams or the music teams are the ones used when church divisions manifest.

The enemy is angry with you for making this choice, be on the alert and like the bible says in Ephesians 6, put on the full armour of God to cover yourself against such. Your challenges will come right from the day you make the choice to start singing for the Lord

Remember also that Gospel music is about Jesus, it's always good to refer back to him on anything pertaining to such ministry. One element Lucifer tries to use is

PRIDE, that's what led to his fall, he knows once he deposits that into you then your fall is imminent

Nomatter how popular you may become, always maintain your humility, be approachable .Your fans and supporters area key to your work, especially those who supported you in the days when you were still a novice. Usually your fame and publicity may supercede that of your pastor because you are on radio and television, BUT REMAIN HUMBLE AND KEEP SUMBITTING. Others, when they become more popular, choose to move to bigger churches and ministries and forget about that small church and that small pastor who offered you rehearsal space and equipment as you started. That family member or fan who would give you transport money to get into town to the studios or to shows. That vocalist who would sacrifice their time and money to travel with you to minister in places where you were only receiving a bottle of water as your token. Greater doors are opened through humility and submission.

Create and sustain a positive image. Remember that you are singing gospel music, which glorifies Christian ideals. Authenticity matters to your audience. Failing to live up to high ethical and moral standards may negatively affect your career. Avoid placing yourself in reckless situations, as temporary fun may lead to long-term career disaster.

Temptations are therefore the order of the day as you rise; these are meant to bring you down. Whilst you should love and accommodate your fans and supporters always, remember to put limits and boundaries. Some of them may be used to tempt and bring you to your downfall, especially in matters of sexual purity and morality. And in Gospel, once you fall its difficult for people to accept you again. Yes God may forgive and accept you immediately because of his love for us, BUT PEOPLE WONT DO THAT EASILY, yet they are the ones who buy your music or attend your shows

Not all Gospel singers may produce instant hits or songs that impact people on a larger scale, you need to be patient. I always refer to my case where even though I started recording in 1998, my big breakthrough came 10 albums later, in 2016! Just put it in your mind that angels will celebrate if only one sinner repents or one soul get uplifted by your song! Before the owner of Gospel music, numbers will not matter, but the accomplishment of the mission will. Don't get discouraged by little numbers, those few that believe in what you are singing and see value in it, should be the ones that push you to keep doing it again and again;

However others may have the grace to start with a bang. The only challenge I have realised with this is you may become famous all of a sudden without having prior experience on how to handle such fame. Also when the chips are down you may be depressed to extents of trying anything...literary anything... to maintain a top echelon placement since you may not be used to low moments in your career.

Always network with those who have been in the industry longer than you, nomatter they made national impact or not. Their experience is invaluable and you may need it to avoid certain traps and paths, as well as use their wisdom a ladder to keep climbing higher

Fame has seasons in the music industry, if you don't make hay while your sun is still shining you nay regret later .At the same time, you also need to read the signs of the times, when the time for your fame to wane and hit-making season starts going down, always have a plan B to fall on. Whilst you are still up there, invest, invest and invest...this is so important because you won't keep getting booked and hired always. Always maintain a great reputation and be nice to those you meet on your way up the ladder, as well as those behind you .Tomorrow you might meet them on your way down, or you might need their help nomatter they may not be as big as you today

Finally, remember it's ALL ABOUT JESUS, never make it yours! This gospel has an owner and if you want to do it excellently, always refer to the owner's manual, which is God's Word as contained in the bible.

Work hard, don't just sit there, or spend your days on social networks either complaining or criticising those who are working hard. Buy the time you realise they have now made it , you will be shocked by where you will still be at. Even though its by GRACE, grace will land and manifest through the work of your hands **(Deut 28:12)**.Work work work, go out there and do what you need to do. God cannot come from heaven to take your songs to studio or to rehearse with your band or even sell your CDs!

May God bless us all as we continue to find ways of overcoming all hurdles and challenges in propagating this gospel though song

GLORY BE UNTO JESUS!

Sources

http://www.virtualpreacher.org/ministry-worship/7-qualities-effective-worship-leader/

www.twitter.com/BradshawBud

http://www.gospelmusic.org/

Eskew, Harry. "Gospel Music, I" in The New Grove Dictionary of Music and Musicians (1980), VII, 549–554.

Malone, Bill C. (1984). "Music, religious, of the Protestant South". In Samuel S. Hill. Encyclopedia of Religion in the South. Mercer University Press.

Patrick, Millar (1962). The Story of the Church's Song. Revised by James Rawlings Sydnor. Richmond, VA: John Knox Press.

Broughton, Viv. Too Close to Heaven: The Illustrated History of Gospel Music. Midnight Books, 1996. ISBN 1-900516-00-4.